THE FRENCH NAVY IN INDOCHINA

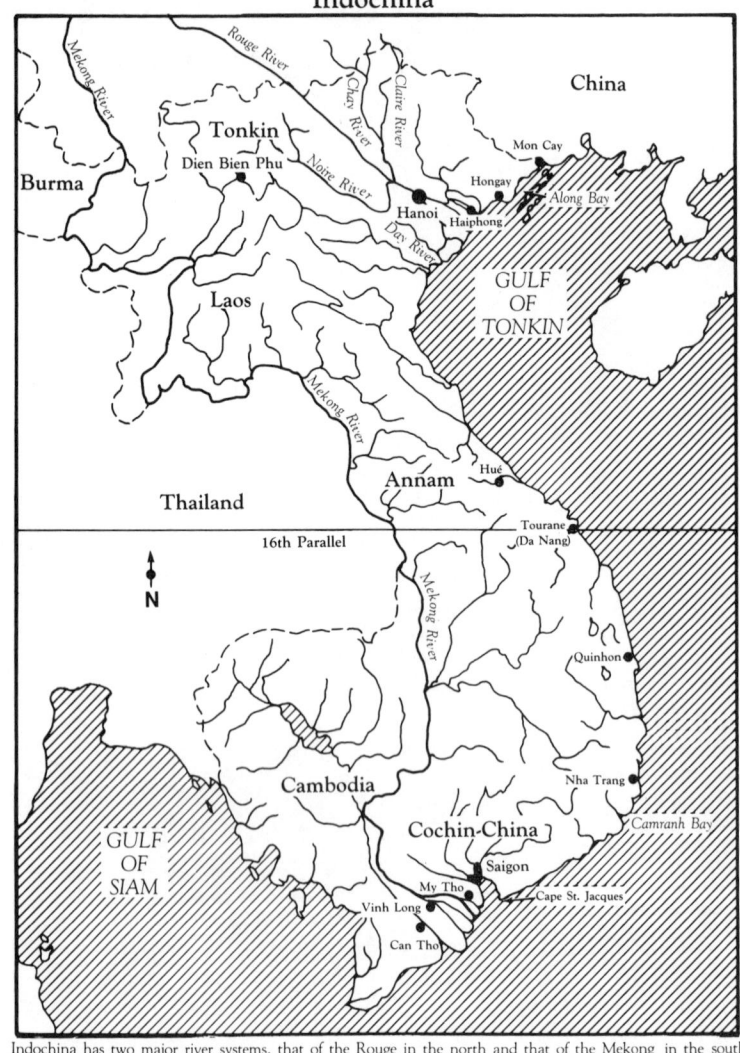

Indochina has two major river systems, that of the Rouge in the north and that of the Mekong in the south.

THE FRENCH NAVY IN INDOCHINA

RIVERINE AND COASTAL FORCES, 1945-54

Charles W. Koburger, Jr.

PRAEGER

New York
Westport, Connecticut
London

Library of Congress Cataloging-in-Publication Data

Koburger, Charles W.
    The French Navy in Indochina : riverine and coastal forces, 1945–54 / Charles W. Koburger, Jr.
        p.   cm.
    Includes bibliographical references and index.
    ISBN 0-275-93833-6 (alk. paper)
    1. Indochinese War, 1946–1954—Naval operations, French.
2. France. Marine—History—Indochinese War, 1946–1954.   I. Title.
DS553.7.K63   1991
959.704′1—dc20   90-23825

British Library Cataloguing in Publication Data is available.

Copyright © 1991 by Charles W. Koburger, Jr.

All rights reserved. No portion of this book may be reproduced, by any process or technique, without the express written consent of the publisher.

Library of Congress Catalog Card Number: 90-23825
ISBN: 0-275-93833-6

First published in 1991

Praeger Publishers, One Madison Avenue, New York, NY 10010
An imprint of Greenwood Publishing Group, Inc.

Printed in the United States of America

The paper used in this book complies with the Permanent Paper Standard issued by the National Information Standards Organization (Z39.48-1984).

10 9 8 7 6 5 4 3 2 1

Les Oubliés du Bout du Monde
(Dedicated to the Forgotten
at the End of the World)

CONTENTS

Illustrations		ix
Introduction		xi
Prologue: World War II		xvii
1.	Reclaiming Their Patrimony	1
2.	No Solution	17
3.	General de Lattre and His Navy	35
4.	The *Dinassauts*	51
5.	Collapse?	69
6.	Dienbienphu and After	81
Conclusion		91
Epilogue		101

Appendix A:	Conceptual Problems of Blue Water Navies	107
Appendix B:	Geography of Indochina	109
Appendix C:	Weather	113
Appendix D:	Abbreviations and Acronyms	115
Appendix E:	List of *Dinassauts* (Sketch Data)	119
Appendix F:	French Aircraft Carriers	121
Bibliography		123
Index		129

ILLUSTRATIONS

MAPS

1. Indochina   frontispiece
2. Mekong Delta   5
3. Tonkin   22

TABLES

1. *Dinassaut* Organization (Basic)   53
2. Selected River Ambushes   65

PHOTOGRAPHS

1. France's Fast Battleship *Richelieu*
2. France's Light Aircraft Carrier *La Fayette*

3. Troops Landing at Van Fong Bay
4. Craft Approaching Ninh Binh
5. French Ex-U.S. LSSL
6. French Ex-U.S. LSIL
7. French Ex-U.S. LSM
8. U.S. LCT(6)
9. U.S. LCM
10. French Ex-U.S. LCM
11. French River Assault Group
12. French LCVPs
13. French Patrol Launches

Photographs follow page 67

INTRODUCTION

Riverine warfare is a convenient term for any projection of raw sea power into inland waters, including rivers that open to the sea. Riverine war is not war *on* the rivers quite so much as it is war *from* the rivers. It calls for special naval organization, equipment, and skills. Improvisation is expensive and usually slow. It can form a crucial aspect of inshore war.

There have been at least five major riverine campaigns in modern times. The operations of the Federal navy on the Mississippi against New Orleans and Vicksburg during the Civil War (1861–65), effectively splitting the South, constitute the first of these. It is the model the U.S. Navy drags out when it wants to show that it knows this kind of war.

Then came Winston Churchill's "river war"—General Kitchener's 1898 campaign of Upper Egypt and the Sudan—although it was fought largely on land and the Nile was but the logistic support route.

The British campaign up the Shatt-al-Arab/Tigris/Euphrates

aimed at Baghdad during World War I (1914–18) was the third. The German operations down the Danube and into Russia and back (1941–45)—classics of their type—count as the fourth. The last took place in Indochina, 1945–75, where the rivers of that peninsula have always been the avenues of access and, frequently, battle zones. It is the first ten years of this long war, 1945–54—the French years—that will concern us here.

There can be no doubt at all that the Western experience in Indochina during the French years was an unmitigated politico-military disaster. This is especially true for the three countries most directly involved—France and its *Marine Nationale*, of course, first with British support, then alone, then later with U.S. aid. This book will do nothing to alter that overall view.

Following the military truism that losers generally learn more from wars than do victors, however, we shall here take a searching look at what the profession of arms might in fact find of lasting worth in the history of French riverine and coastal forces in that ten-year conflict. This should prove of continuing value. The profession is neither outdated nor dead. Take a look at today's paper.

Any serious reading in the history of that war will soon show that the one thing naval historians seem to agree on is that the French-developed (and later U.S.-exploited) *dinassauts*, or naval infantry assault divisions, are one such contribution. We would be foolish to let the idea of these most successful river assault groups fall between the cracks of history and, after all that has occurred, be lost to us.

Dinassaut in French actually means *division d'infanterie navale d'assaut*. *Dinassaut* is a convenient French military acronym. It marked this era.

In the midst of the ashes and the gall of defeat, there were for the proud French a few bright coals—these *dinassauts*. The French navy in Indochina successfully performed every task given to it—coastal patrol, river patrol, and river assault—doing even more than was expected of it. To the riverine *dinassauts* belongs most of this credit, and they can here symbolize the rest.

INTRODUCTION

This book does trace the overall course of the Indochina war, but only with sufficient political and military detail to allow the reader to place the naval story in context. It tracks the whole story of the navy in Indochina, too, for the same reason, but in somewhat more detail.

It should be noted here that we are not making moral judgments on French colonialism. That has always been an emotion-charged subject with Americans, and in any case is beyond the purview of a book like this.

This book will then concentrate on an account of the French development of such river assault groups and review some of their tactics and techniques. It will recount some of their battles, and examine the outcomes. It will salute some of the brave men who made the *dinassauts* such a success. Americans were the inheritors of their work.

INSHORE WARFARE

This is, in the end, a book about naval strategy—one very particular aspect of it. This is a book about riverine and coastal warfare, the ability to wage which is often essential to any true exploitation of sea control. For sea power to have any broad, relevant meaning today, it must always be projectable at least from the sea to the shore and up the rivers and canals onto and into the land.

Consciously or not, the United States' Captain Mahan blinded Americans to this. He was, of course, writing in 1890 for and about "blue water" high-seas navies—big ships, big guns, large fleets, each fighting the other over great distances. The Spanish-American War (1898) neatly validated his ideas.

Britain's Admiral Fisher found Mahan just when he most needed to give conceptual meaning to his pre–World War I concentration in the North Sea of the Royal Navy's far-flung ships. They thus managed to keep a tenuous command of the sea.

Allied victory in World War I "proved" Mahan's theses. Ignored or forgotten immediately were the subsidiary little wars around the world, wars that called for entirely different kinds of ships—smaller, shallow-draft minesweepers, submarine chasers, gunboats, and transports.

World War II saw Neptune as god, Mahan his prophet, and the U.S. Navy as the only true church. Again, the United States won. American inshore warfare capability was then dismantled as quietly and as quickly as possible. Available resources were devoted to supercarriers for a supernavy ready to fight World War III.

As one result, there is in the U.S. Navy a sharp, clear, immediate knee-jerk reaction to any idea of retaining a permanent, significant inshore capability. Any such heretical diversion of (scarce) resources takes away from the supernavy. The thought often brings what amounts to dismay—covered by unnecessary anger—to naval officers.

Forgotten are Korea (1950–53), Vietnam (1965–73, for the United States), and the Persian Gulf (1987–88), in all of which Americans had sooner or later to improvise an inshore capability. In Korea, mines kept the United States out of Wonsan. In the Persian Gulf, it took the United States a year to get its escort act together. In Vietnam—more directly relevant to this book—it might be said it took three years to organize a proper riverine force.

People live ashore. Naval blockade alone is expensive and usually slow in taking effect. Occasionally, it is of no effect at all. Sea power today must be able to affect people. It must, therefore, reach up the inland waterways to where they live. An effective, efficient inshore capability is an essential component of sea power.

Indeed, there have been several good books about U.S. riverine and coastal warfare in Vietnam, some even published by the U.S. Naval Institute. But these have done little to produce a permanent, significant U.S. inshore capability. The French have had as much trouble with this as the Americans (see Appendix

A). Perhaps this book will help overcome this continuing strategic shortfall.

ORGANIZATION AND ACKNOWLEDGMENTS

This book then will be a simple one, perhaps a little technical, of primary interest to those who continue to do their duty as it is set out by their political masters. Naval and marine officers will find it of most use, but the other services who want to broaden their professional horizons should also find it of worth. So will military historians. And politicians. And veterans of U.S. involvement in riverine Vietnam.

The organization of the book is also relatively simple. The first part sketches the situation in French Indochina as it was in August and September 1945, with emphasis on the naval picture. It then describes the origin of the *dinassauts* and their first crude operations. They did not, after all, spring whole out of the mind of some staff officer. Rather, it was operational logic that drove them.

The next part covers the long development of the French riverine and coastal forces, especially that of the *dinassauts*, as the French navy learned to use them, adapting material available to hand. This period stretches from 1946 to 1950, and describes the riverine and coastal strategy then employed by the French.

The third part deals with the expansion of *dinassaut* operations made necessary by the communist victory in China, and made possible by expanded U.S. aid to the French navy. Covered are the years 1951 and 1952. Riverine now becomes estuarine.

The final part describes the last years of the French in Indochina, sketching the culmination of the *dinassaut* organization, and highlighting a few of their last operations. It summarizes French tactics, and evaluates their ultimate role. Both the interim Vietnamese and the Americans built on what the French had done.

Throughout, only enough of the overall military picture is given for the reader to follow a coherent story. It has been well covered elsewhere. A detailed survey of Indochinese geography and weather is given in appendices for the serious. It is, after all, the riverine and coastal forces we are going to concentrate on. Included is an account of the conceptual problems riverine warfare caused the French.

Names and their spellings have troubled me. In the end, those employed in this book are those in use by the participants at the time, only occasionally adjusted for at least minimum consistency. They are admittedly a mixture of French, Vietnamese, and English. Any attempt to further rationalize these names—for instance, to convert them all to modern, 1990s Vietnamese—would serve only to add to the reader's confusion and cut him off from the available sources.

The technical aspects of the various landing ships and crafts mentioned in this book have been only briefly sketched. This is a narrative history. To have covered the landing craft in detail would have fundamentally changed its character. There are just too many ships and craft. See Appendix D for types. Several good reference works are listed in the Bibliography for further study of this aspect.

Many people helped form the idea of this book and encouraged the writing of it. The U.S. Naval Institute purchased an earlier manuscript on the French navy in Indochina during World War II, but thankfully has never published it. I have since learned much more about what happened, and I hope now that they do not. The institute also gave me permission to use material from some of their earlier publications on the subject.

Retired French Rear Admirals Alex Wassilieff and H. Labrousse both encouraged and helped, each in various ways. So did M. Philippe Masson, noted French naval historian, who gave much of his valuable time.

There is no escaping the fact that the author alone is responsible for this book and for any possible errors it may contain.

PROLOGUE: WORLD WAR II

THE WORLD TURNED UPSIDE DOWN

World War II was the historical watershed for the French colonial empire, as it was for that of the British and the Dutch, in Indochina as elsewhere. Before then French interests were all on the upswing; after that their days were numbered. To fully understand what follows, it is necessary to begin with World War II. It sets the stage for a look at subsequent events.

As German *panzer* troops rolled swiftly eastward across the golden wheatfields of Poland in September 1939, France gathered itself for war. At first only distant echoes reached the Far East.

In 1939 French Far Eastern naval forces consisted of two cruisers (heavy *Suffren* and light *Lamotte-Picquet*), eight old flying boats, four assorted colonial gunboats, two submarines, three hydrographic vessels, and seven river gunboats. Some of these ships were detailed to Chinese waters, a few served in the Southwest Pacific, but most were based in Indochina, at Saigon (main base), the anchorage at Camranh Bay, and Haiphong.

Overall responsibility for the defense of Indochina rested with the French governor-general. He was assisted in this matter by a "council of defense" comprising the chief military and naval authorities.

One of the few immediate results of the outbreak of the conflict in Europe was the appointment in 1939 of an outstanding officer, General Georges Catroux, as governor-general of Indochina, replacing the former civilian governor.

With the defeat of the *métropole* in Europe and the resulting armistice, in 1940, Indochina was isolated, blockaded by the British, cut off from replacements and reinforcement. The foundation of France's maritime strategy gone, Indochina was left to wither.

One of the navy's two cruisers (*Suffren*) departed Indochinese waters in 1940, never to return. The other (*Lamotte-Picquet*) and the four old colonial gunboats were soon formed into an open-ocean force of sorts. It was the open-ocean force that took on a superior Thai fleet, destroying or damaging the greater part of it, defending Indochina's western provinces. These ships were then gradually laid up, mined, or wrecked. Guns were salvaged, crews put on other tasks.

A few of the river gunboats were new, purpose-built ships. Most, however, were tired old submarine chasers left over from World War I. They had not been included in the open-ocean force, and they continued to show the French flag up the farthest waterways, sometimes with little more than dew under their keels.

The breakdown of French military power in Europe was the signal for Japan to make strong representations to the colonial government concerning the transport of munitions to the Nationalist Government of China. The traffic had been going through Indochina via Haiphong for several years. The collapse in Europe combined with Japanese demands occasioned a major crisis in the colonial government, and General Catroux finally resigned and fled. He was replaced as governor-general by skillful Vice Admiral Jean Decoux on July 20, 1940.

At the end of June, Tokyo further demanded the right to land forces in French Indochina. Japanese warships arrived at several ports and stayed. In July the French informed Tokyo that the transport of arms through Indochina had been forbidden by decree and had been stopped. Japan then demanded the right to station military inspectors at appropriate points to watch the roads from the port of Haiphong to the Yunnan border. The French were in due course forced to agree, under the greatest duress.

In September, Japan abruptly demanded permission to move troops to and from South China via the road from Haiphong to Yunnan and Kwangsi. Before agreement could be effected, there occurred a series of incidents that could hardly have been accidental and in which Tokyo blatantly laid bare its ultimate intentions in the Land of the Three Kingdoms, as Indochina was then sometimes called.

Toward the end of the month, Japanese troops from the army in Canton suddenly seized the military post at Dong Dang on the French Indochinese border, some 120 miles north of Hanoi. The next day they attacked the French troops at Langson, in a full-scale assault. Meanwhile, in Hanoi, only 82 miles away, agreement finally had been reached allowing limited Japanese forces to enter Haiphong and the northeast corner of the country.

Early in March, the Japanese exacted the right to occupy the airport at Saigon, within bombing distance of Singapore. One of their land-based naval air fleets moved in at once.

In June 1941, the Vichy government, now helpless, announced that it had granted a Japanese demand for complete military control of French Indochina. The agreements, which took effect in July, gave Japan the right to station an army of 40,000 troops in the country and granted it access not just to the north but also now to the whole area, including the south. Virtually all French military establishments and facilities were turned over to the occupying troops as they moved in.

The Japanese proceeded rapidly to organize the three kingdoms (Vietnam, Laos, Cambodia) as a base for the lightning thrusts against Thailand and Malaya that were preliminaries to the full-scale assault on Singapore, to follow the December 7th attack on Pearl Harbor. The French were immobilized and throughout the rest of the war contented themselves with maintaining the civil administrative structure, what equipment the Japanese had left them, and keeping internal order.

A slight, inspired Communist by the name of Ho Chi Minh had by this time become the acknowledged head of the native resistance movement against the Japanese. He was, in the course of events, forced to flee into South China. There, in 1941, he gathered other Indochinese, nationalists of all types, and organized them into the Vietnam Independence League, best known as the Viet Minh.

On December 7, 1941, the uselessness of Singapore and the hopelessness of the Allied cause in Southeast Asia were demonstrated by air attacks mounted in Saigon and other airports of Indochina. A Japanese force invaded Thailand and, by December 9th, had occupied Bangkok without firing a shot. Camranh Bay in Annam became an important staging area for Japanese operations toward the south.[1]

THE JAPANESE LEGACY

The tense, explosive charade in Indochina broke wide open early in 1945. Conscious that Decoux's administration was still intact, and of the liberation of metropolitan France the year before, the Japanese were nervously aware that the U.S. build-up in the Philippines might well indicate an amphibious Allied assault on Indochina. Some of the more farseeing leaders in Tokyo were also becoming aware of the inevitability of their defeat. They decided first, in any case, to complete the destruction of the French in Indochina.

On March 9, 1945, the Japanese handed Decoux a blunt two-hour ultimatum demanding complete Japanese administrative as well as military control of Indochina. When the authorities delayed, stalling for time, the Japanese quickly ordered their forces into action. Some of the French garrisons were surprised and surrendered without a struggle. Others, both French and Vietnamese, warned in time, put up such a bitter battle and made the affair so costly that the infuriated Japanese massacred some of the units to a man.

On March 9, 1945, almost everything the French navy had left was either seized, scuttled, or destroyed by gunfire. Their crews were made prisoner, brutally herded into prison in Saigon under the most primitive conditions. Only two small armed former customs launches—*Frézouls* and *Crayssac*—managed to escape, hiding out in the bays, creeks, and swamps of northern Tonkin and southern China. Captain André-Jean-Baptiste Commentry, SNO Tonkin, was one of those not caught in the Japanese net. He fled Haiphong with some 100 men, rallying Port Wallut, on the island of Ké Bao at the northern end of the Fai Tsi Long chain. There he found *Frézouls* and *Crayssac*, the two launches, and was joined by other naval escapees such as the armed junks *Audacieuse* and *Vieux Charles*. Commentry kept the tricolor flying, at least here.

Decoux himself was arrested by the Japanese, his dogged five-year defense of French interests in Indochina collapsed around him. Decoux was never to resume power.

The Japanese, in attacking the French civilian cadres as well as the military structure, totally destroyed them as instruments of government. The French colonial presence was discredited and wiped out.[2]

Indochina still had to be governed. The Japanese could not and did not want to attempt this directly. They declared instead an "independent" Empire of Vietnam and appointed as their puppet and emperor a man named Bao Dai. Bao Dai had been emperor of Annam (1932–45). Born a prince, he was the son of Annamese emperors. Since Annam historically ruled Indochina—when it was ruled—Bao Dai was for the Japanese a logical choice. Hué was his capital.

Things were never, however, going to be that simple. There was at least one other major power center, not legitimate and not under Japanese control.

In the meantime, Viet Minh columns, numbering hardly more than 10,000 ill-armed men, taking advantage of the confusion, occupied most of Tonkin. They had little assistance from Chiang Kai-shek, but did receive small amounts of American weapons parachuted to them and some American technical advice. Japanese resistance was slight.

In August 1945, seizing his opportunity, Ho Chi Minh issued a call for a general insurrection. In the turmoil that again resulted, Emperor Bao Dai abdicated and the pro-Japanese puppet government resigned. On the 25th of August, Ho was able to proclaim the Vietnam Democratic Republic, making Bao Dai his "supreme advisor." A week later, Ho Chi Minh entered Hanoi at the head of a communist-dominated coalition government of all parties. The new republic theoretically included Tonkin, Annam, and Cochin-China; Hanoi became its capital.

Before the total collapse of the Japanese, the Viet Minh set up the framework of an effective de facto independent government for the entire country. Thus the already defeated Japanese left the French the difficult task of reconquering peoples who had already been permitted their political freedom. To complicate the problem, they themselves contributed a number of arms to the Annamese nationalists.

WAR'S END

On August 15th, island Japan, strangling on a sea and air blockade and twice hit by atomic bombs, surrendered, ending the Pacific war. China was temporarily to occupy the northern half of Indochina, maintaining order until a post-war government could be organized; British forces were to occupy the south. Little real help was offered the French by the Allies—divided as to policy—to return.

From the earliest stages, although not as a matter of priority, however, the British stated that they intended to assist the French in resuming control of the region. As soon as the French were strong enough to maintain law and order, British troops would

PROLOGUE

withdraw and transfer all military and civil functions to the French. By mid-August several bilateral Anglo-French agreements had already been signed, reflecting this understanding.

By mid-September, the French had designated their key leaders for post-war Indochina. The senior French political official, holding the title of high commissioner, was Vice Admiral Georges-Thierry d'Argenlieu. The overall military commander (commander in chief) was to be Lieutenant General Philippe Leclerc. Neither was yet in place.

The abrupt ending of World War II presented the communists in Indochina with a tremendous opportunity to seize power. Surviving French military forces were not released by the Japanese but kept prisoner. Munitions and other supplies were seized by the communists. A full month would pass before the initial arrival of Allied liberation forces. Still more time would pass before these forces would be strong enough to assume effective control.

The British reached Saigon in mid-September by air. Saigon was in chaos. The forces available to the British were extremely limited, but they immediately ordered the release of the French prisoners. This made available a small French contingent of approximately 1,200 men, including a provisional naval battalion (Lieutenant Commander Picheral, commanding) of two companies of four sections each, culled from the fittest of the old ships' crews. These the British immediately put to work.

The old hands ("*les anciens*") of the naval battalion were for the most part nothing but scarecrows dressed in rags and tatters. Their feet were bare, their shoes locally made sandals. Their weapons were a miscellany of former French ones kept hidden from the Japanese or recovered from them, too few, in any case, and with little ammunition or spare parts.

Most of the men had been in Indochina at least since 1940. These old hands were suffering from dysentery and malaria, malnutrition, and physical abuse by the Japanese. Yet they had retained their military cohesion. Their performance now was impeccable, their gallantry superb.

In at least one case, the hard-pressed British found the assistance of the naval battalion invaluable. On the 28th of September at the Chinese Arroyo, the Viet Minh were about to overrun a British Indian unit. The battalion rushed up and helped the Dogras disengage from the ambush, saving the day.[3]

The first large increment of French reinforcements debarked at Saigon on October 3rd. This 1,000-man force consisted of units brought from Ceylon in two British transports—*Princess Beatrix* and *Queen Emma*—escorted by French fast battleship *Richelieu* and destroyer *Triomphant*.[4] Several landing parties drawn from the ships' companies also went ashore at this time.

The French—like almost everyone else—had been caught short by the peace. They had certainly contributed considerable naval forces to the Allied Indian Ocean effort, but they had little else there of any immediate use in Indochina. To bring any significant numbers of troops to Indochina, basically their Indian Ocean ships had to steam back to France, pick up the troops, and then carry them back to the Far East. This all took time, and time was what they had least of.

The major French force designated for Indochina was a Far East Expeditionary Corps, formed June 15th. It was to be composed of one armored and two colonial infantry divisions, under the direct command of Leclerc. This corps included a sizable naval component, the Far East Naval Brigade (*Brigade Marine d'Extrême-Orient*, or *BMEO*), about which more as we go. The corps had been destined to take part in the final assault on Japan.

The various elements intended to make up the expeditionary corps were scattered widely, some in France and North Africa, others in Ceylon, Madagascar, and even China. Their assembly would still take a while, even under the best of conditions.

The naval forces and their leaders were similarly spread out. Rear Admiral Gaston-Elie Graziani, commander-designate of the French navy in Indochina, was only to join in mid-October. Vice Admiral Philippe-Marie-Joseph-Raymond Auboyneau, commander in chief-designate of the French Naval Forces Far East (not just those in Indochina), joined only at the end of November.

Meanwhile, Captain Commentry—who had been out to Paris to report and who had come back on September 12th with British General Gracey—took over as NOIC. He acted as commander of both the Saigon naval arsenal and what French naval forces there still were.[5]

General Leclerc, his staff, and the first advance elements of the new reinforcements from France reached Saigon on October 5th. As the month wore on, other components continued to arrive. They came on a wide assortment of French ships, using whatever was available to them: transports *Ville de Strasbourg* and *Quercy*; an old aircraft carrier now turned transport, *Béarn*; cruisers *Gloire*, *Suffren*; destroyer *Fantasque*; destroyer escorts *Somali* and *Sénégalais*; sloops *Annamite*, *Gazelle*.

Lieutenant General Jacques-Philippe de Hautecloque, called Leclerc, was not an easy man to deal with. He had little time for either the navy—that included the BMEO at first—or the old Indochinese hands. He expected his armored division to do most of the pacification. But Indochina was not France or the western desert, where he had made his name as a general. Here there were people, rice paddies, jungles, swamps, mud, and water—lots of all of them.

The attitude of the returning French is well summed up in a statement made by General Leclerc, when he landed at the airport in Saigon to assume military command. "We have come," he said, "to reclaim our inheritance."

By early December, French military personnel—still concentrated in Cochin-China—had swelled to 21,500. The British force totalled some 22,000 officers and men. The British kept order in Saigon and along its route to the sea. The French continued to work to extend their control throughout the countryside, using Saigon as their base.

NOTES

1. Paul Auphan et Jacques Mordal, *La Marine Française dans la Seconde Guerre Mondiale* (Paris: Editions France-Empire, 1976), pp. 286–87, 306–9, 562–64.

2. Paul Romé, *Les Oubliés du Bout du Monde* (Paris: Editions Maritimes & d'Outre-Mer, 1983), pp. 160–76.

3. Ibid., pp. 211–13.

4. The two transports were former Dutch cross-Channel steamers converted during the war to carry amphibious assault units together with their landing craft.

5. Georges Thierry d'Argenlieu, *Chronique d'Indochine 1945–1947* (Paris: Editions Albin Michel, 1985), pp. 22–42, 51–52.

1

RECLAIMING THEIR PATRIMONY

FAR EAST NAVAL BRIGADE (BMEO)

By December 1945, the Far East Naval Brigade—the first elements of which had disembarked at Saigon on October 19th—began to take recognizable shape. Commander François Jaubert—the senior brigade officer so far to arrive—assumed temporary command of BMEO and acted directly under Leclerc. Jaubert had been charged with setting up the framework of the brigade at Arcachon (France, southwest of Bordeaux), utilizing personnel from the 3rd and 5th Naval Infantry Regiments[1] as cadre. He thus was already known to Leclerc.

It was originally expected that BMEO would fight ashore in the role of a regimental combat team, as they had done in France. There were to be two battalions of infantry, one of tanks, a naval commando, a battalion of artillery, plus staff, administration, and services. That was definitely not the way things worked out.

Commander Jaubert was an exceptional chief, a great organizer and improviser, highly intelligent, interacting easily with all kinds of people. He was one of the few naval officers to make a favorable impression on the famous but difficult general. He was to exploit this.

Jaubert had soon demonstrated the necessity in Indochina of some kind of riverine force, and as we shall see, BMEO was to become the father of the *dinassauts*. Geography (two large deltas, lots of water), the nature of the new enemy (savage, ruthless, river-dependent), and the task at hand (pacification) all combined to make a riverine force indispensable.

Most lacking at the moment were suitable ships and craft. The old French river gunboats were all sunk now. The navy's new war-built sloops could cruise the Mekong estuary, but they could not operate in the creeks that twisted throughout the delta and that were the only real avenues of penetration into the interior.

Jaubert made and continued to make do with what he could find, requisitioning unhesitatingly anything river-worthy. Especially sought after was anything that could work up the twisting creeks, most especially anything that could be put to work right away and that could be called self-propelled. Jaubert sent officers scrounging for river craft, motors, weapons, spare parts, and docks. He also sought a river base.

He set up his headquarters in the former Saigon Yacht Club, across the Arroyo de l'Avalanche. He even put a statue of Buddha in the main hall, invoking the protection of the local god for his flotilla.

Within a few weeks, Jaubert had obtained and armed five small vessels, including two former Japanese junks acquired from the Royal Navy, and an assortment of three craft captured from the Viet Minh. Then he had to put his craft into operational shape and find crews for them.

Several motorized junks were thus manned by a mixed bag of seamen of all specialties, assembled from a variety of sources, not always very qualified to operate them. They all learned, little by little. Almost everything was makeshift and lashed together in those days. The French—racing time, desperate to fill the political vacuum—made do.

DELTA OPERATIONS—THE IDEA

Commander Jaubert soon put his hands on a real find: several motorized barges belonging to the Gressier rice firm. These barges were flat-bottomed boats with a metal hull. They had been designed to carry some 200 tons of rice each, at the tremendous speed of four knots, up from the rice fields of the Bassac to the rice mills of Cholon.

These barges were the most primitive of craft. Abandoned and neglected in a corner of the port, they were covered with rust and partially stripped. The hulls were paper thin. The coxswain's position was totally open, without shelter from the weather. There were no facilities for the crew. It was never certain whether the Bolinder motor would start, and if so, ahead or back. They were in very poor shape.

Lieutenant Paul Romé—who had actually located these barges—discovered that one could be made immediately usable. Romé took her out and began ferrying troops across and along nearby waterways, thereby changing the essential nature of riverine warfare for all time.

These Gressier barges, once modified and refitted, rearranged internally, protected, and armed, were to render exceptional service during the next several years (1946–47). They were given names like *Lave, Dévastation, Tonnante, Volcan,* and others, names taken from the armored barges France employed in the Crimean War.

Personnel from the provisional naval battalion, if fit, were immediately incorporated into the naval brigade, as planned. Few except the seriously ill could be allowed to go home until overall French strength was sufficiently built up. Some of the old Indochina hands had not been home for five years or more.

Some among the new arrivals were Gaullists, a rank or two above their classmates. There was initially some arrogant distrust of the old hands ("Vichyites") among them. But once the record became clear, and new problems were faced together, that naturally tended to disappear. At the working level, anyway. In the end, manpower was always in desperately short supply, and such stupidities could not long be tolerated. They all needed each other too much.

In these early days, the naval brigade, operating basically ashore, cut its teeth by helping complete the liberation and pacification of the Saigon area. As that task wound down, they moved out to operate as a true riverine unit, primarily in the Mekong delta.

Those rusty old Gressier barges—having been specifically designed for these waters—could go anywhere, almost. For short distances they were capable of carrying a whole rifle company complete with its equipment. They were thus capable of landing troops ready to attack a strong point; to hit a flank, relieving pressure on another unit; to occupy and hold ground; or to block or close off given areas.

The barges also carried out a number of auxiliary chores. They brought up food, fuel, and ammunition. They evacuated casualties. They acted as unit command posts, until command could be shifted ashore. Once armed, they provided a source of independent fire support.[2]

In short, those barges were a godsend. The French were not slow in getting the idea. They began at once to improve on it.

PROVING THE IDEA (OPERATION *MOUSSAC*)

Now, the immediate task of this new riverine amphibious force—initially designated the Naval Infantry River Flotilla—was to reestablish a permanent French presence along the Bassac and Mekong rivers.[3] That was done at once.

The next objectives of the Naval Brigade in the Mekong delta were three strategically located provincial capitals held by the Viet Minh. These were all towns of from 45,000 to 80,000 people. The first to be taken was My Tho, situated at the juncture of several

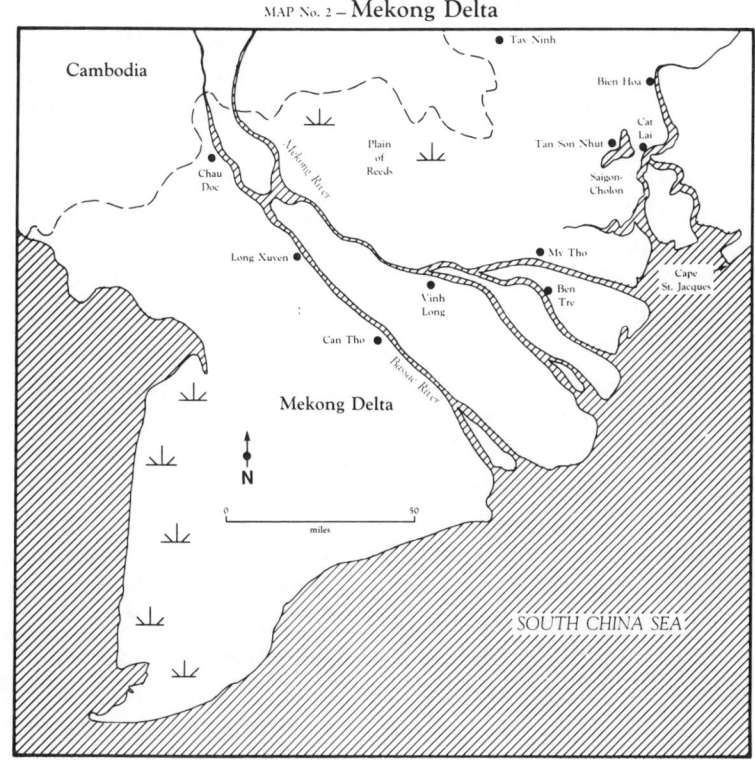

MAP No. 2 – Mekong Delta

highways, on the north bank of the main shipping channel to Phnom Penh (Cambodia) (see Map 2).

Operation *Moussac* was begun October 24th. For this operation, the Royal Navy was to provide landing craft to transport themselves and another 270 French troops by water.

My Tho had initially been assigned to a combined force of army units moving out overland from Saigon. However, the French column found the road cratered and the bridges blown. For their tanks and trucks the going was impossibly slow. Their vehicles were forced to attempt to go around or to ford the endless obstacles, but they had great difficulty just leaving the road, never mind moving across country. Infantry did little better. Thus, contrary to original plans, the reoccupation of My Tho during the last week in October was actually effected by units of the brigade. By the time the army column reached My Tho, it had already been captured by a force of naval commandos led by an officer named Pontchardier, coming in over water on small river craft, supported by sloops *Gazelle* and *Annamite*.

That same week, in a joint operation with army units advancing overland—through the paddies, in the mud, across streams—another contingent of the brigade embarked in *Annamite* took control of Vinh Long, and held it.

Then on October 30th, a 90-man force from the brigade overcame Viet resistance at Can Tho and captured that town. The small force had a tiger by the tail, however, being surrounded by swarms of guerrillas. It could not remain passive. Operating out of Can Tho, the French force actively conducted patrols, ran ambushes, and raided down the river to give the impression that it was larger than it actually was. It also succeeded in holding on.

By mid-November—after a second unit of the Naval Brigade arrived in country—the French were able to extend the pacified operational area out to a 25-kilometer radius from Can Tho. They seized four smaller towns and villages, capturing quantities of useful ammunition and equipment.

It had been the same to the north of Saigon. On October 15th, a small Franco-British combined force—one British LCI (landing craft, infantry) and French destroyer *Triomphant*—was dispatched to occupy Nha Trang, on the coast. Therein also hangs a tale.

When a 60-man French landing party entered the city, the Viet Minh demanded it leave. It stayed. On the 22nd, the Viets attacked it. Their attack was beaten off and the town cleared. Later in the month, *Richelieu* arrived off the port, ready to support the landing party with her guns. By early November, additional French forces had arrived, and Nha Trang appeared secure.

Nevertheless, the enemy controlled the roads into the city, and maintenance of the French position in Nha Trang depended on support from the sea. It was to be three months before the army fought its way up Route Coloniale No. 1 into town.

THE COST

Mass reprisals, individual murder, rape, torture, fire, and pillage were to be a mark of the Viets all through the time of the French, and beyond. They were used as a conscious political tool. They helped isolate the French and their local allies, the village chiefs, the doctors, the school teachers, the police, the military.

Such behavior on the part of the rebels accomplished many things. It helped further destroy the myth of the white man. It vented desires for personal revenge. It bound even those who only watched passively more tightly to the rebel cause. Somehow they all became guilty. In this war, there could be no innocent bystanders.

This was all clear right from the very start of the war. During the course of one of these early operations in the delta, BMEO came across the remains of one of their earliest convoys, missing since November 18th. The find was a shock, the news of which was passed throughout the brigade. The real nature of the campaign was gradually being made clear. The story is as follows.

On the 18th, a tug towing several junks, with an armed guard of some 20 men, simply disappeared. The convoy had departed My Tho for Saigon, but was never heard from again. Error of navigation or duplicity of a local pilot? No one knows.

The missing convoy had been caught in a small creek and completely shot up. The lucky ones died at once. The others had been tortured to death, their bodies atrociously mutilated and hastily buried in a nearby mass grave. It was going to be a long, hard war.

FRUITION OF THE IDEA

On Indochina's extensive coastal and riverine waters, riverine warfare was to come to its fruition. There could no longer be any real doubt. Inescapably, here the navy's general transport mission was to continue to the end, but the initial combat successes won by the naval brigade in its own right had undoubtedly impressed General Leclerc. As early as November he had directed the Brigade's brilliant acting commander—Commander Jaubert—to establish within the force a permanent flotilla of small boats and a self-contained naval infantry landing force. This force was to be capable of undertaking sustained autonomous operations throughout the delta.

In early December ubiquitous aircraft transport *Béarn* delivered a flotilla of 14 landing craft, assault (LCA), and six landing craft, vehicle and personnel (LCVP), purchased from the British at Singapore, the first of many such. These landing craft were armed and gradually armored. They were given the names of the "*petites amies*" of certain of the naval officers and petty officers in charge, names like *Doudou, Ramatou, Vahine, Sampanière,* and *Marinière.*

Small boats, junks, and a variety of small ships still provided field living quarters for Jaubert's force.

BMEO at this point comprised two companies of naval infantry (a total of about 400 men), augmented by a small detachment landed from *Richelieu* and *Béarn.* Throughout December, while preparing for extended campaigns, these units helped to mop up around Saigon. Organization and training were begun. A second river flotilla was formed. Doctrine development was initiated.

So were the *dinassauts* born.[4]

On December 19th, the British transferred responsibility for administering the Saigon region to the French, completing a process begun a month earlier. Subsequently, the British turned over to the French the former British naval headquarters plus a number of additional landing craft (LCAs, LCIs, and LCTs). They were all put to good use.

RIVERINE OPERATIONS

Subsequent operations of the Far East Naval Brigade are of the most interest to us here, and it is these that we shall continue most closely to follow. By January 1946, the naval brigade had reached a strength of some 3,000 officers and men. Captain Robert Kilian had assumed command. Its naval infantry was the heart of the brigade and would remain so. Small parachute-trained naval commando units had also joined.

In addition to the normal troop units, BMEO manned their transportation and support: about 50 landing craft assembled from various sources and perhaps 30 assorted junks, scows, and launches obtained locally.

There was the usual staff, although the continuing scarcity of personnel kept it down to a manageable size. Included also were specialist communication, repair, river base, and medical elements.

In the beginning there were no permanent marriages between naval infantry and their transport. The floating units were used wherever, to move whatever. Whatever often meant army troops, for whom the naval-manned transport was a godsend. In the delta, movement across country by foot was a nightmare of water, mud, and ambush.

As time went on, however, and cooperation with the army continued, it became somewhat routine. It was more and more limited to large joint operations requiring manpower beyond that organic to BMEO, and available. Otherwise, *Fusilier Marin* commandos carried the *dinassaut* load.

Cooperation with the army was not always as easy as it should have been, especially with units unused to working with the *dinassauts*, for the high command was in army hands. Staff discussions could get quite heated because, for instance, army officers did not understand that in tidal areas the twice-daily tides determined navy planning timetables in an imperious fashion.

In the early days, even operational army units failed to understand that in tidal areas, unless they kept strictly to their orders, landing craft could easily be left high and dry. Later, however, the army itself established tide tables for their sectors.

This tended to reinforce BMEO's already strong inclination toward the permanent marriage of specific *Fusilier Marin* units with specific flotillas. Some flexibility was admittedly surrendered, but performance in this specialized warfare was as a result much more expert, and casualties lower.[5]

The successful outcome of these French operations enabled the British to implement the planned withdrawal of their forces in Indochina. On January 1st, 1946, a statement issued jointly by Admiral Mountbatten and Admiral d'Argenlieu proclaimed that from then on the French would have sole responsibility for maintaining law and order throughout southern Indochina.

INTO ANNAM

A major campaign, launched in January 1946 by nearly all elements of the expeditionary corps, followed. It had as its objective control of the land lines of communication reaching north from Saigon into Annam. In order to secure a reliable base from which to support these operations, the Far East Naval Brigade—then almost at full strength—was assigned the mission of securing the rivers and canals to the northeast and east of Saigon. The largest operation was an advance up the Don Nai River and its tributaries, from January 20th to 25th. Involved were two armored barges, eight landing craft, and amphibious assault forces, all drawn from Commander Jaubert's Naval Infantry River Flotilla.

On the 25th, aggressive, imaginative Commander Jaubert was mortally wounded while gallantly directing an attack from a launch north of Saigon. Despite this, the transportation routes north into Annam were successfully opened.

French army and navy units subsequently conducted a successful series of operations along the central Indochinese coast, supported from the sea and along the rivers. By the close of the first quarter of 1946, the major population centers and lines of communication in Cochin-China and Annam south of the 16th Parallel were in French hands. In a major sense, this was largely thanks to the efforts of the navy.

Attention was now turned to reoccupation of the Phu Quoc Islands in the Gulf of Siam, and of Poulo Condore, off Cape

St. Jacques. Sloop *Gracieuse* and an LST were involved. At Phu Quoc, the (only) *Fusilier Marin* platoon landed during the night to secure the beachhead, guided by fire from the sloop. The bulk of the force landed the following dawn. There was no resistance. At Poulo Condore, everyone walked ashore. There was no resistance there, either.

As the French continued to build up their forces in Indochina, they reached the point where they were too strong to resist the temptation to continue using them. They were, however, never strong enough to keep the rebels from trying to solve their political problems by throwing the French back into the sea. The test was soon to come.

PRELIMINARIES IN THE NORTH

Above the 16th Parallel, the situation was more difficult than in the south, insofar as the French were concerned. The Nationalist (Kuomintang or Chungking) Chinese had been given responsibility for enforcing the peace here. They may have had territorial designs on the north. They did loot the area of everything they could move. In any case, they did not particularly welcome the return of a European colonial power on their southern border.

The initial effort to reestablish the French position in the north was made by the two small navy-manned ex-customs launches— *Frézouls* and *Crayssac*—that had escaped capture at the time of the March Japanese coup de main by taking refuge in Along Bay, along the Tonkin coast. There they had fought a lonely little campaign of their own, finally being forced temporarily into China (Pakhoi). On August 11th, they were back in Hongay at the bottom of the bay. On the 15th, they showed up off Haiphong, proudly flying the tricolor.

On the day after Hirohito had issued his ceasefire order (the 15th), the two craft (Lieutenants Blanchard and Vilar commanding) determinedly steamed up the river to Haiphong. Garnier had done no less. There they first grounded, then were held, shot up by the Viet Minh. After two tries Blanchard was able to reach Hanoi by road, using a Japanese escort. Alone, however, he was unable to do much. He could not obtain the release of French military personnel still held prisoner by the Japanese, as in the south. It was only on October 5th that the French were finally released.

Crayssac was, however, betrayed to the Viet Minh on September 4th at Hongay. She was then in the course of carrying out a medical evacuation under the Red Cross flag. Lieutenant Vilar was murdered in the process.

Faced with *force majeure*—open Nationalist Chinese and Viet Minh opposition to the establishment of any substantial force in the heartland of Tonkin—subsequent French military operations during 1945 were concentrated in the coastal regions.

For several months, the French were represented in the north only by a small base at Port Wallut and tiny isolated posts in the Fai Tsi Long archipelago, supplied precariously by patrol boats and several armed junks. Otherwise these craft put down the rampant piracy, one being captured by *Frézouls* on September 3rd, for instance.

In mid-November, the arrival of destroyer escort *Sénégalais*, later relieved by *Somali*, then *Algérien*, allowed the French to consolidate their position in the archipelago.[6]

Special attention was devoted to securing Along Bay because of its extensive and exceptionally sheltered anchorages and its harbor, Hongay. The lower end of the bay, 20 miles east of Haiphong and 70 miles southwest of the Chinese border, was a natural base for further operations as the French came north.

RETURN TO THE NORTH

The principal theater of action now shifted from south to north, and there it was to remain for nine more years. On February 28, 1946, finally, the French Ambassador to China and the Chinese Foreign Minister reached agreement in several separate but interconnected accords. In these accords, the French made a number of concessions concerning Chinese use of Haiphong and the Red River for trade purposes. These were the price the French paid to get the Chinese out of Tonkin. The Chinese were to be gone by the end of March.

Meanwhile, the French navy was assembling at Saigon and other Indochinese ports almost all its Far Eastern forces. These were prepared for an amphibious landing in the north, to replace the Chinese. Available were three cruisers, seven destroyer types, a transport group of eight ships (including *Béarn*), and a unit of two LSTs and eight LCIs ceded by the British, as well as numerous LCTs, LCAs, and similar craft.

Operation *Bentré* was certainly the most important amphibious operation the French navy had up to then mounted by its own means. By February 28th, loading of 21,700 troops—including the newly designated Northern Tactical Group of the naval brigade—along with their arms, ammunition, vehicles, and equipment was essentially completed. *Béarn* at Cape St. Jacques had taken aboard elements of the 9th Colonial Infantry Division. The French force got under way for Tonkin the following day. The 6th of March would be the last day for two weeks in which tides would be high enough to permit these ships to transit the Haiphong channel.

Meanwhile, parallel negotiations were under way in Hanoi between Jean Sainteny—acting for d'Argenlieu—and Ho Chi Minh concerning the future status of Indochina. Sainteny reached an agreement with Ho the same day that the French flotilla steamed up the Haiphong channel. The agreement was preliminary and provisional, but it did accept the relief of the Chinese forces by the French, and it did recognize a Republic of Vietnam as part of the French Union.

That same day, however, as French landing craft reached a point in the channel approximately 2,000 meters east of Haiphong, the Chinese unexpectedly opened up on the French force with intense artillery and small arms fire. The French ships returned the fire and temporarily pulled back down the river. Following hasty Sino-French local discussions on board *Triomphant*, on the

7th the French were allowed to begin to land, on the island of Haly, called by the natives the "Island of the Dead." Not until the 16th, however, would the Chinese allow French troops to enter Hanoi. It was actually midyear before the last of the Chinese were gone.[7]

On March 8th, in a separate Anglo-French agreement, the British turned over to the French all their remaining duties. By April, the last of the very helpful British were gone. By the end of August, the last of the Chinese were gone. The French now faced the Viet Minh one-on-one, in a growing crisis. The French kept building up their forces.

Thus war came to Indochina again. During World War II, defeated France's position in the Far East proved untenable. Undermined first by Japan's occupation, finally destroyed by them, then by the Viet Minh, after liberation France initiated emergency efforts to regain control. In the beginning, the French had British support, but that was now finished. Nationalist China, supposed to be an ally, was at best passively neutral and even permitted Ho Chi Minh to govern in the north during its occupation there.

The rebellious Viet Minh, in the hills and swamps of the south and in Hanoi in the north, were not prepared to accept a return to colonial status. They had a coolly calculated plan of action all prepared. What this plan was, how execution was initiated, and how it was put down will be considered in the next chapter.

NOTES

1. Naval Infantry (*Fusiliers Marins*) trained for amphibious assault operations similar to those undertaken by the marines of other navies. The French navy contained no separate marine unit.

2. Paul Romé, *Les Oubliés du Bout du Monde* (Paris: Editions Maritime & d'Outre-Mer, 1983), pp. 224–29.

3. It was not until 1947 that the term "*dinassaut*" was actually used. This sometimes appears as *DINASAU*.

4. Robert McClintock, "River War in Indochina," U.S. Naval Institute *Proceedings* (December 1954).

5. Robert Kilian, *History and Memories: The Naval Infantrymen in Indochina* (Paris: Editions Berger-Levrault, 1948), passim.

6. Paul Auphan et Jacques Mordal, *La Marine Française dans la Seconde Guerre Mondiale* (Paris: Editions France-Empire, 1976), pp. 580–81.

7. Ibid., pp. 582–83.

2

NO SOLUTION

INTERREGNUM

Up to December 1946, although there had been considerable hard fighting between Ho Chi Minh's Hanoi government and the French, there was yet no formal state of war between them. The French seem to have hoped for a compromise solution-by-negotiation to the Indochinese problem, but were generally unaware of the seriousness of the situation, and were then unwilling to make any real concessions. For many Frenchmen, trapped by history, Indochinese politics in 1945–46 was little changed from that of 1873–74; they were about to be disabused, the hard way.

Ho's government and d'Argenlieu's French danced a very careful minuet around each other. Ho visited the French fleet off Haiphong, where he was honored by a review. He was invited to France (Fontainbleau) for discussions on Indochina's future. But

Ho was not willing to give up anything of worth, either.

Ho's writ did not always run in the south. There were deep, long-standing political and cultural differences between the two areas, and the south was considerably more under French control. Some in Cochin-China even had thoughts of a separate government of their own, ideas that may have been encouraged by the French but that naturally infuriated Ho.

Beginning in October 1946, a series of incidents was initiated by the Viet Minh, carefully designed to provoke French retaliation and bring an end to the uneasy truce on terms favorable to the Viets. In December, Ho succeeded.

FORMAL WAR

In the north, a lengthy dispute with maritime implication—control of Haiphong customs—was reaching a critical state. To prevent the continued smuggling of communist war supplies through this major port, and to dry up a major source of funds with which additional materiel could be bought, in October the French seized control of the customs from the Viets by force. The French also instituted armed patrols—a blockade—to cut off Viet Minh supplies coming in by water. This is back in 1946, remember.

On November 20th, in Haiphong, a small French patrol craft seized a Chinese junk carrying contraband cargo. When the French patrol was fired on, heavy fighting between the Viet Minh and the French broke out.

On the 23rd, in the name of security, the French issued an ultimatum to the Viet Minh demanding that they evacuate specified areas of Haiphong. The Viets failed to comply, and so eventually French ground and naval units moved in to take the positions and clear the city by force. The supporting French naval bombardment inflicted unintentional and unavoidable but heavy casualties (according to communist propaganda, as many as 6,000) in the native quarters of the city. The trap had been sprung. If the situation had ever been resolvable by negotiation, it no longer was.

On the 19th of December, in Hanoi, the Viet Minh responded with their own coup de force. There they cut off the utilities, blowing up power stations and sabotaging water systems. They assassinated French and pro-French civilians and attacked police and military posts, in an orgy of fire, pillage, torture, and rape.

French forces this time repulsed the communists only after several days of very heavy fighting. In the end, of course, they succeeded in reestablishing firm control of the city. By the 23rd, the city was under martial law and French tanks patrolled the streets.

Unlike the Haiphong affair of the previous month, which remained an isolated incident, the Viet attack in Hanoi was accompanied this time by similar outbreaks of trouble elsewhere in Tonkin as well as in Annam and Cochin-China. Smaller battles took place in a dozen towns north of Hanoi and on the coast at Hué and Tourane, where French reinforcements had also been landed. A war that was to last eight years was now under way, with no turning back.

During the latter part of December, the French moved back into the north in force. Ho Chi Minh fled Hanoi and went into the Viet Bac hills on the Chinese border. These he made his primary politico-military base for the remainder of the war.[1]

From there, Ho now concentrated on building up his political infrastructure throughout the country. First, patient propaganda, then sabotage, terrorism, and finally guerrilla warfare were orchestrated to separate the people from their legitimate government at the point of contact, substituting that of the rebels.[2] For now, Ho concentrated on avoiding fights he did not think he could win, meanwhile building up his regular forces.

Gradually, the countryside was mobilized. It was then integrated into the communist military structure. No single villager was left unlectured, untasked, or unrecruited in some form. While the population was organized, and local militias formed, the political work continued and the political base extended.

INSHORE ORGANIZATION

French military operations in the war against the Viet Minh were always shaped to a large extent by geographical considerations and maritime capabilities. France could easily bring troops, equipment, and supplies in by sea and move them from one point to another on the long, indented coastline, projecting them ashore and up inland waterways by amphibious and riverine efforts. Within extensive areas of Indochina, movement by water far exceeded that by land. Naval ships and craft could extend control over major water routes and the traffic that flowed on them and intercept enemy movements along coastal waters. The limiting factor was always the composition and size of available naval forces.

Under Commander in Chief French Naval Forces Far East—then Vice Admiral Philippe Auboyneau—the main fleet units were assigned to Commander Naval Division Far East. In December 1946 these were three heavy cruisers, three colonial sloops, four minesweeper-corvettes, four frigates, and one division of minesweepers. Auboyneau's other major subordinate was Commander French Naval Forces Indochina. This officer commanded approximately 100 ships and craft, ranging in size from 192-foot LCTs to 50-foot LCAs and small native craft. He also had the Far East Naval Brigade. It was here that Indochina made its greatest impact.

On January 1, 1947, the Naval Amphibious Force was organized under Naval Forces Indochina. It had two flotillas, one in Tonkin and one in Cochin-China. All of the khaki navy was now assigned to one amphibious flotilla or the other.

Most of BMEO's *Fusilier Marin* units—except for the naval commandos—had already been broken up. The men manned instead the landing craft and river patrol boats being used for the support and transport of the army. The commandos were considered elite troops even by the army. Five sections of commandos were assigned to Tonkin and two to relatively—only relatively—quieter Cochin-China.[3]

French naval officers writing of this period often recognized the similarities between the then current operations on the inland waterways and those undertaken by such naval trailblazers as Garnier, Rivière, and Courbet in the 1870s and 1880s. Some few of these operations were mounted up the shorter rivers flowing into the sea along the Annamese coast. A greater effort was devoted to the waterways of Cochin-China. There a particular concern was the protection of civilian convoys carrying rice and other supplies into Saigon. But the most crucial riverine region was Tonkin, where the Viet Minh had always had their greatest strength and the level of combat was usually the most intense (see Map 3).

NAM DINH

Now, in December 1946, when full-scale hostilities erupted in the north, the city of Nam Dinh was among those most threatened. Nam Dinh, with a population of perhaps 70,000, was the third largest city in the north, after Hanoi and Haiphong. It was located in the delta southeast of Hanoi, on the Red River. Nam Dinh was held by a garrison of about 500 men. There was a French civilian population of between 200 and 300 people.

As Viet Minh attacks—determined, intense—continued, it became obvious that the evacuation of the civilians and the reinforcement of French forces were imperative. After considering the hazards of an overland relief—as well as the time this would take—the French developed a plan for a coordinated assault and relief by riverine and airborne forces from Haiphong.

The naval forces were commanded by a Lieutenant François. His flotilla consisted of two LCTs, one LCI, and four LCMs (landing craft, mechanized). To it was assigned the basic task: transporting the artillery, tanks, supplies, fuel, food, ammunition, and reinforcing infantry to the beleaguered garrison. The relief force was expected to arrive via the narrow Nam Dinh Canal, adjoining the Red River, at dawn on January 6, 1947. Some 400

MAP No. 3 – Tonkin

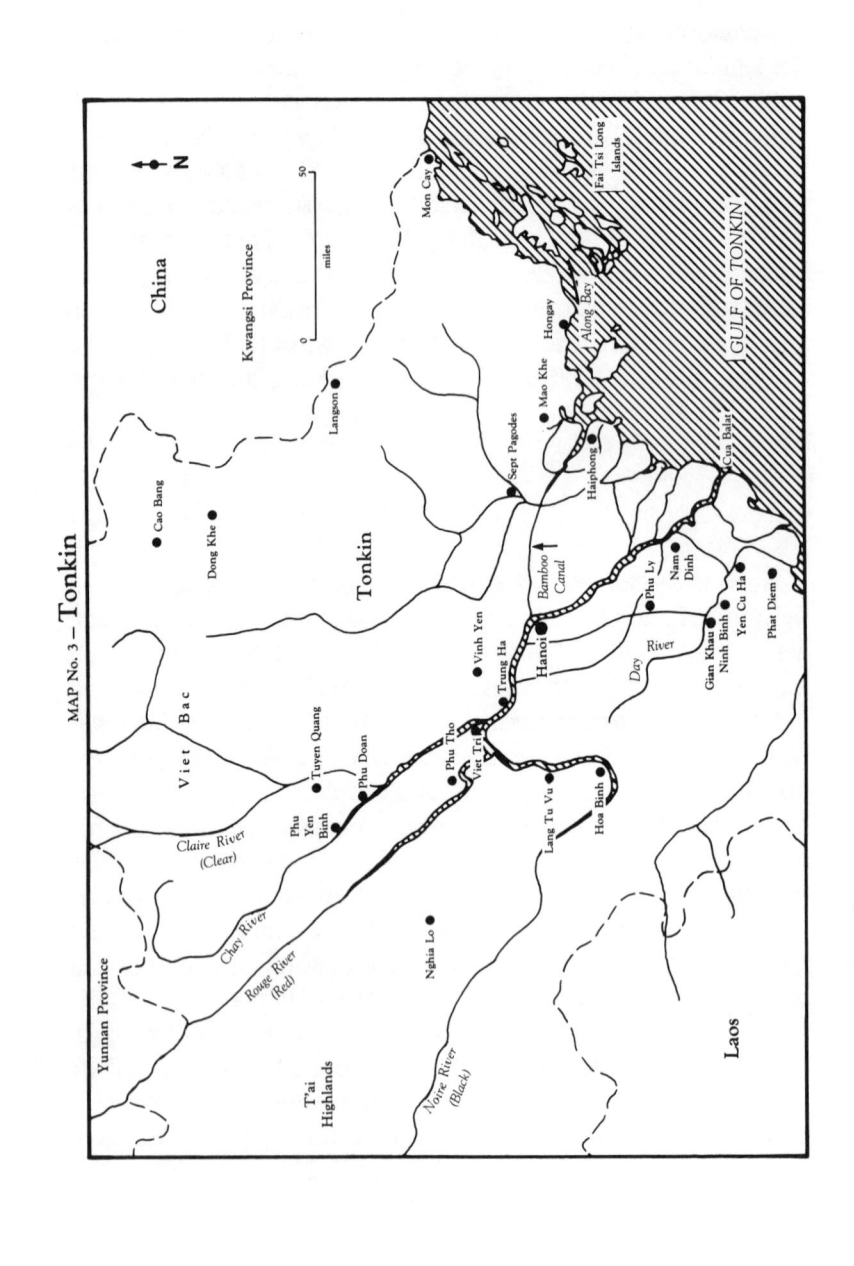

airborne troops were scheduled to drop some hours earlier, with the task of establishing two beachheads on the canal where the flotilla could land its troops and cargo.

The most direct inland water route from Haiphong—the base—to the Red River was the Bamboo Canal. However, this waterway lay in a region controlled by the enemy. The expedition's commanders elected rather to enter the Red River at its mouth, on the gulf.

What happened next was to become typical of many subsequent operations in the north. Sailing from Haiphong on the night of January 4th, the flotilla narrowly succeeded in crossing the shallow bar at the mouth of the Red River at high tide on the following morning. Beyond lay the enemy, which ambushed the convoy at several points during the passage upriver but failed to halt it. Early on the morning of the 6th, under cover of darkness and heavy fog, the flotilla neared Nam Dinh.

The parachute elements met with heavy antiaircraft fire, and their preparatory drop was only partially successful. The airborne force became widely scattered, and it was unable to secure the designated beachheads.

As the flotilla approached Nam Dinh, therefore, heavy enemy fire erupted from both banks of the canal, sinking one LCM and killing François. Under these conditions, Lieutenant Garnier—worthy of his predecessor—succeeded to command of the flotilla. Seeing that enemy fire from the far side of the canal, across from the intended landing points, was somewhat less intense, he landed his troops there. He supported these troops with heavy gunfire from his landing craft. Within a short time, the enemy's positions on that side of the canal were silenced. The French then concentrated their fire against the opposite bank, from which the enemy soon fled. By noon, the way for the entry of French forces into Nam Dinh had been cleared. At 1630, its mission accomplished, the flotilla departed for Haiphong, taking a number of French civilian evacuees with it.

The successful completion of the mission did not by any means end the navy's involvement at Nam Dinh. In March, two additional supply and reinforcement convoys were successfully dispatched to the city, despite repeated enemy ambushes. Thereafter, there were regular monthly or bimonthly convoys to Nam Dinh. Although such logistic support was recognized as essential, these recurring operations absorbed a large percentage of the navy's resources in Tonkin, often precluding assault operations elsewhere in the north.[4]

AMPHIBIOUS OPERATIONS

When the Viet Minh launched their offensive in December 1946, the port city of Tourane just north of the 16th Parallel was threatened and the French forces there placed in jeopardy. As was the case years later when American forces were deployed to the area, the major road and railway connections to this region were among the first targets of the Viet Minh, who easily obstructed the land routes by destroying bridges or excavating whole sections of the highway.

The situation in the Tourane area was brought under control by troops brought in by sea and supported by gunfire from ships of the French navy, including heavy cruisers *Suffren* and *Tourville*, during the period December 20, 1946, to January 8, 1947. Once the security of that city was assured, the French mounted a series of amphibious operations to recapture Hué, then held by the Viet Minh. These landings were undertaken despite the seasonal peak of the northeast monsoon, which brought periods of rough seas, pounding surf, and limited visibility.

Between the 18th and 21st of January, the French navy landed troops at four separate points north of Hai Van Pass, where the road and railroad from Tourane to Hué hug the coast. More than 1,500 troops were landed under the protection of naval gunfire, and supplies built up for the overland advance to Hué. Then, on the 4th of February, the second phase of this operation began, when a flotilla of ten landing craft, with troops embarked, entered the lagoons separating the approaches to Hué from the open sea.

A frontal assault by the landing force and French army columns moving up from the south led to the recapture of Hué by the 9th of February.

Over the next two months, equally successful amphibious operations were launched in the Fai Fo region, just south of Tourane, and at several points on the southern Tonkin coast. By the end of March, the French had reestablished control over most of the major population centers along the coastal sections, although the Viets still controlled pockets in the area.

Air support of an amphibious assault at Fai Fo on the 16th and 17th of March, 1947, marked the first combat use of aircraft carriers in French history. The ship from which the missions were launched was ex-British escort carrier *Dixmude*. Four hundred ninety-two feet in length, 8,200 tons, with a maximum speed of 16.5 knots, she carried SBD-6 Dauntless dive bombers, obsolescent but reliable, a dozen of them.

Dixmude furnished close air support for the Fai Fo operation for the first ten days, then moved north into Tonkin Gulf. On April 2nd, her aircraft struck Viet Minh base areas near Tuyen Quang, a road junction in the mountains northwest of Hanoi. Very useful she was.

Thus, in her first actions, *Dixmude* had demonstrated the importance of a carrier's ability to move freely from one area to another and concentrate air power wherever it was needed. Such a capability was particularly important in Indochina because of the small numbers of air bases ashore and their limited facilities for supporting combat operations.[5]

RIVERINE AND COASTAL OPERATIONS 1947–49

In October 1947, the French launched an offensive—Operation *Lea*—intended to deal the Viets a decisive blow. Specific goals of Operation *Lea* included capture of the Viet leadership, destruction of the main force of communist regular troops, and seizure of positions that would facilitate the resealing of the Chinese border. This huge operation, one of the largest ever launched by the French in the whole war, if successful in reaching its geographical targets, failed to destroy the enemy who vanished into the extremely broken terrain.

A parachute assault on the Viet headquarters in the Viet Bac failed to capture Ho Chi Minh or his general, Vo Nguyen Giap. The subsequent advance into the Viet Bac failed to contact the elusive communist main force, which avoided engagement. A combined amphibious and ground thrust up the Clear and Red River valleys into northwestern Tonkin did succeed in securing pockets of territory for the French, but again the enemy's principal forces largely eluded them. Only in northeastern Tonkin, at the border town of Cao Bang and other points along Route Coloniale No. 4, were objectives achieved.

As a point of fact, the French never regained continuous control of the Chinese border. Operation *Lea* was the first of a long series of swift but never-decisive French victories. Nonetheless, the French kept trying.

GIAN KHAU

A more successful French operation was carried out early in 1948, when a naval force composed of four LCMs and two LCAs loaded two companies of army troops and naval commandos and set off to raid Viet positions near Gian Khau. The objective, 65 kilometers from the *dinassaut* base that had been established at Nam Dinh, had to be approached via the Day River through territory infested with enemy.

Nevertheless, moving under cover of darkness the force achieved strategic if not tactical surprise. On February 2nd, with minimal opposition, landing parties swept through four enemy villages, destroying a number of Viet installations.

The morning of the 3rd, after anchoring in the Gian Khau area overnight, the force began its return back down the river, fully expecting an ambush. To meet this threat, the French deployed their force in two columns, with the LCAs 500 meters in advance of the LCMs. The lead boats were instructed to watch the banks for evidence of the controlled mines used by the Viets. In the event of attack, the officers in charge of both types of craft were directed to land the embarked troops on the enemy's flanks at once; at the same time, every gun was to open heavy fire into both known and suspected Viet positions.

At exactly noon, the anticipated ambush was sprung. Viet positions were scattered on both sides of the river. The French executed the planned response with great skill, achieving excellent results. Within 20 minutes, the Viets were driven off with losses of more than 100 men and a significant number of weapons.

This had been, however, a search and destroy mission, not one to clear and hold. Once the French had left, the Viets came back. Every so often, somewhere, the process would be repeated.

RIVER PATROL

In this period, colonial sloops were still employed on the Mekong and on other large river estuaries. These 630-ton sloops were recognized as being vulnerable when near shore, so they were essentially used for rapid liaison, as a base of fire (they carried two 90-mm guns), and as an element of prestige.

Substituting more and more for these traditional sloops, however, especially in the upper reaches of the large rivers and on the smaller ones, were *vedettes de patrouille* (VPs). These wooden-hulled, 82-foot motor launches were manned by a crew of 12. Their two engines gave them a maximum speed of only 12 knots, but twin propellers and twin rudders made them very maneuverable to make up for it. For patrol boats, they were armed to the teeth, carrying two 20-mm guns, two heavy machine guns, one mortar, and one light machine gun. At creep speed, they were very quiet boats.

COMAR Mekong, a commander in rank, was based at My Tho. In charge of these VPs, he had his own LCI (landing craft, infantry), using it to move around to inspect or support. His problem was typical.

VPs—commanded by lieutenants (junior grade)—were often given responsibility in the Mekong delta for policing patrol sectors as much as 150 kilometers in length. In the "forbidden zones," entirely under the domination of the Viet Minh, the VPs had total freedom of action. These were free-fire zones. Only major events were required to be reported. Here, all junks and sampans met were destroyed to prevent their further use by the Viets. Prisoners taken from them were immediately released on nearby riverbanks, providing, that is, that they carried no arms or documents. In the latter case, they were turned over to the army.

VP personnel were forbidden to take action ashore in these zones. However, de facto landing parties of the officer in charge and four men were not unknown. They were modern day corsairs, these men.

In the cleared areas, on the other hand, river traffic was protected, the VPs only attempting to intercept cargoes of arms.[6]

IMPASSE

So, the French military continued its traditional efforts to pacify the country, retaking in November 1948 the once thriving Sontay in the Red River delta. Out of an original local population of 6,000, only seven people and one church were left when the French reoccupied the town. This was success?

As a consequence of actions such as these in the deltas and along the coast, the initial communist attacks against population centers were repulsed and overrun positions were promptly regained by French forces. Giap withdrew his troops to remote inland regions, where he built bases to prepare for guerrilla warfare and the development of regular army units. He continued to use the Viet Bac for his main base area and established smaller bases in the provinces of Thanh Hoa, Nghe An, and Ha Tinh— south of the Red River delta. In addition to providing safe areas for the training of troops, the small-scale manufacturing of munitions, and the stockpiling of arms, these base areas were also the location of political and administrative headquarters and indoctrination units.

Militarily, the chief problem of General Marcel Carpentier, then commander in chief, was still to clear the communists from the country's rich food-producing areas and centers of population in the deltas. This would at one stroke cut off the rebels from food and recruits. These operations routinely involved the riverine and coastal forces.

France also now had to prevent somehow a firm junction between Ho's forces and the approaching Chinese communists. By airlift and truck convoy, it was the army that worked to maintain the old line of forts—Laokay, Cao Bang, Dong Khe, Langson—at the passes along the northern border. Their logistic support came up the rivers, protected by the navy as far as they could go.[7]

This next period is relatively empty of large-scale battles. Rather, there were many small unit actions, slowly escalating skirmishes which the French generally won but which ate away at their men. The Viets all the while kept burrowing industriously into the Indochinese polity, using a combination of persuasion and fear.

ARROMANCHES

At the end of 1948, the arrival of *Arromanches* off Indochina showed again the major contributions aircraft carriers could make in a limited war. *Arromanches*, a light carrier, had been lent to France by the United Kingdom in August 1946 for a five-year period. With her full-load displacement of 18,000 tons, length of 695 feet, and speed of 25 knots, she was more stable, with a longer flight deck, and faster than escort carrier *Dixmude*. She was far better suited for combat operations than *Dixmude*, but still small enough for easy inshore work.

Making full use of her mobility during even a short time on station—from November 29, 1948, to January 4, 1949—*Arromanches* and her Dauntless squadron carried out as many air support and strike sorties as had been flown by the entire French air force in Indochina during all of 1948.

Thanks to her inherent mobility, the carrier was able to select launching and recovery points almost anywhere in the Tonkin Gulf. The running trade-off was fuel and ordnance, determined by distance to target. In Indochina, these were ordinarily not major factors. *Arromanches* was thus able to avoid the worst of the northeast monsoon weather, conditions that often grounded land-based air units.[8]

CRISIS

Nonetheless, by the end of October 1949, the French High Command had no choice but to order an emergency regrouping of forces. In 1946, a French squad could go anywhere it was sent. In 1947, it took a platoon; in 1948, a company. By 1949, it took a battalion to intervene ashore, and then sometimes even a battalion was not strong enough.

In March 1949, minesweeper *Glycine* had disappeared while on river patrol. Her hulk was later discovered beached up a narrow arm of the river. The sweeper had been mined. Only one of the 36 on board escaped. Her commanding officer, his officers and crew were seized by the Viets as they swam ashore, and paraded from village to village until publicly tortured and massacred.

The French had gradually become overextended. It was now decided to concentrate in the north on defending a perimeter extending 160 miles around Hanoi—containing a population of over 200,000—and nearby Haiphong. In so doing, General Carpentier would gain shorter lines, simpler routes of communication and supply, terrain in which artillery and tanks could be used to better advantage, and where strong, extensive naval support would be within reach.

Until this time, the French, insofar as the United States was directly concerned, were on their own in Indochina. Impoverished France—struggling to recover from the effects of World War II and the German occupation and beset with troubles elsewhere—

had repeatedly sought U.S. arms, munitions, naval ships and craft, and other military equipment. Although support was provided to assist metropolitan France, sales that appeared to relate to Indochina were never approved.

With Mao Tse-tung's proclamation of the People's Republic of China on October 1, 1949, and his November occupation of positions along the Tonkin border, the United States began to reverse itself. When Ho proclaimed his Democratic Republic of Vietnam, Mao—on January 18, 1950—recognized it. On January 20th, the U.S. Joint Chiefs of Staff recommended that a provisional $15 million be allocated for political and military aid to the embattled French. The USSR added its recognition of Ho's government on the 30th, dutifully followed by other communist countries. In Indochina, the new lines were being drawn.

In the spring of 1950, the United States decided to grant military aid to the French fighting in Indochina. The navy members of the joint State-DoD mission sent to survey French needs judged that the objectives of seagoing forces should be as follows:

—to prevent delivery by sea of outside assistance going to the Viets;
—to carry out combined operations against enemy-held coastal regions, including amphibious landings;
—to ensure the flow of supplies to French forces.

Riverine forces were required, too, for the following uses:

—to deny Viets the waters;
—to interdict enemy logistic traffic;
—to protect French use of the rivers and deltas;
—to enable the French to conduct combined operations there and from there.

The French desired that the U.S. Navy block off Tonkin Gulf and the South China Sea to enemy forces that might come south to attempt landings in support of the Viet Minh, in addition to whatever direct military aid the United States sent. The blue water tasks were to be for Americans, the white and brown water ones for the French.[9] This proved to be the outline for continued Indochina naval policy for the next four years.

THE NEW LINES

Nonetheless, by late November 1950, there were few immediate results to be seen. After seven continuous weeks of success, Ho's army had closed up to the French in the Red River delta. There the French forces were outnumbered two to one. Against Ho's 70,000, the French could field fewer than 40,000. The remainder of the French army of 165,000 either were garrisoning southern Indochina or were on the staffs and in the services.

To add to the army's problems, even inside the delta were hidden pockets of communist troops, in some places (inside Hanoi) at battalion strength, 600 men.

The main axis of the new defensive system in the delta was a road, Route Coloniale No. 5, railway, and power line running straight from Hanoi to Haiphong. Crossroads, especially of lateral routes, were occupied by mobile reserves theoretically ready to pull out to any threatened place on the delta's edge.

The valiantly defended French posts on the northern frontier, monuments of another age, all that stood between the Viet Minh and the communist Chinese, thus collapsed one by one. The French could now possibly keep the Viet Minh from winning, but the French themselves could not now win. They also could very easily lose, first the delta, and then all of Indochina.

The first of December 1950, therefore, the best that could be said about the issue in Indochina was that it was in doubt. The Viet Minh, everywhere successful, had pushed the French into a corner in the Red River delta and the French had not, up to then, found a way to stop them. They *were* stopped, if only for the moment, and by one man.

As the French withdrew into the Red River delta, there to remain for four years more, the war entered a new phase, even became a new war. Communist China was now at the border in strength, ready for Ho with sanctuary, arms, ammunition, and training areas. The war was no longer colonial. It had become internationalized. The United States responded with massive military aid.

This new war will be the subject of the following chapter.

NOTES

1. Georges Thierry d'Argenlieu, *Chronique d'Indochine 1945–1947* (Paris: Editions Albin Michel, 1985), pp. 369–78.

2. Roger Trinquier, *Modern Warfare* (New York: Praeger, 1964), passim.

3. Robert Kilian, *History and Memories: The Naval Infantrymen in Indochina* (Paris: Editions Berger-Levrault, 1948), pp. 227–38. Hervé Jaouen, *Marin de Guerre* (Paris: Editions du Pen Duick, 1984), pp. 61–70.

4. Jacques Mordal, *The Navy in Indochina* (Paris: Amiot-Dumont, 1953), pp. 208–17.

5. Edwin B. Hooper, Dan C. Allard, and Oscar P. Fitzgerald, *The United States Navy and the Vietnam Conflict: The Setting of the Stage to 1959* (Washington, D.C.: Naval History Division, 1976), pp. 129–31.

6. Ibid., pp. 131–33. Jaouen, op. cit., pp. 77–92.

7. Mordal, op. cit., pp. 284–91.

8. Hooper, Allard, and Fitzgerald, op. cit., p. 134.

9. Edwin Bickford Hooper, *United States Naval Power in a Changing World* (New York: Praeger, 1988), p. 211. The naval part of the plan worked to the end. When the French—exhausted—were forced to pull out in 1954, the United States itself gradually took over the whole plan.

3

GENERAL DE LATTRE AND HIS NAVY

GENERAL DE THÉÂTRE

It was in Paris that this next remarkable phase of the war in Indochina began. There, early in December 1950, Premier René Pleven offered the collapsing command at the end of the world to politically powerful, very able, flamboyant General Jean de Lattre de Tassigny. Unhesitatingly, this man, whose niche in France's history was already conceded, accepted.

The French MacArthur, de Lattre was sometimes known irreverently as General "de Théâtre." In an egalitarian age which tends to denigrate the essentially unquantifiable value of leadership, de Lattre was a towering figure, a fact that he was to prove once again at the bottom of the world.

Not every general (or admiral) can be a humble soldier. The only absolute is that they have to win their wars. Anything less is foolish. Such generals are scarce.

French regulars were already fully committed. By law, French draftees were forbidden to serve outside the *métropole*. Further significant reinforcements therefore being out of the question, France sent a man.

De Lattre departed for Indochina with a crucial advantage over his predecessors: there was now for the first time to be complete unity of command. He was to wield plenary power, with both political and military authority, something which heretofore had been divided between the high commissioner and the military commander. The general was to have full control over the military, the civil power, and the various police. He could fight. He could negotiate, and fight. He could offer terms. This chapter is about him.

MARINE INDOCHINE IN 1950

By 1950 there were substantial (12,000) French naval forces committed to Indochina. The French had gained experience, too, and their overall Indochina organization had been refined in light of it. This organization reflected the greater sophistication of their effort, also, as the *Marine Nationale* as a whole became more fully aware of all the implications of the Indochina effort.

Naval Forces Far East (*Forces Navales en Extrême-Orient*, or FNEO), although directly subordinate to the theater commander— C in C Armed Forces Indochina—was responsible for the entire naval effort in the Far East. Under Commander FNEO himself there were two intermediate echelons of command—Naval Forces Indochina (the two amphibious forces, south and north) and Naval Division Far East (the larger open-ocean "blue water" ships). This was not too different from the past.

Headquarters FNEO was located in Saigon, as was the major naval base. Haiphong had a secondary base, the support center for the north. Along Bay was a major anchorage, as was Camranh Bay. This too reflected the past.

Air base capabilities ashore were still very limited. At the time, there were major airfields only at Saigon, Bien Hoa, and Hanoi.

There was one additional smaller air base at Haiphong. These were adequate for current military operating levels, but not for expanded efforts.

There were of course airstrips elsewhere—at Tourane, for instance—but their expansion was extremely difficult. Solid, flat, dry land in the deltas and along the middle coast was always hard to find.

In just five years of hostilities, however—1945–50—the fundamental character of that part of the French fleet operating under combat conditions in Far Eastern waters had radically changed. Such change had been a matter of need and necessity, but it made some of the higher naval leaders uneasy.

FNEO had begun in 1945 as a recognizable fragment of a traditional high-seas fleet led by new fast battleship *Richelieu* and counting at one time or another a maximum of one small aircraft carrier, as many as three cruisers, two destroyers, three destroyer escorts, six transports, and three sloops. There were numerically not a terrible lot of them, but they were "real" ships.

Reduced to a famine budget, the navy in Paris had been forced to withdraw most of the big ships one by one. *Richelieu* had been recalled early, decommissioned, and placed in reserve. She had not been replaced. There was now no battleship and only one light cruiser on scene to furnish major naval gunfire support. There was an apparent effort to begin providing carrier-borne air support.

By the middle of 1950, FNEO had indeed increased to approximately 165 ships and craft. French naval personnel totaled about 12,000, 10,000 of whom were assigned to the riverine, amphibious, and logistic components. The seagoing forces now included only one combatant of destroyer size or larger (that light cruiser), and seven major auxiliary ships (one transport, two oilers, one repair ship, three LSTs). A small carrier had begun to appear intermittently on station. The balance of the French forces was composed of patrol and landing craft, minesweeping units, and utility types.

It had been the dust on the sea—the landing ships and craft—that had been built up, at the same time that the big ships were drawn down. This fed back on the whole navy. The need in such a war for far fewer big ships and many more smaller ones did not go unnoticed on Paris's Rue Royale (the Navy Ministry), or in Toulon or Brest.

Approximately 40 of the landing craft had been joined with naval commandos to form six *dinassauts*—all a very tight budget would at this point allow—two of which continued to operate in the normally quieter delta regions of Cochin-China and Cambodia and four in turbulent Tonkin.

French ships and craft all operated under one regional command or another. For coastal and riverine activities, under the operational control of Commander Naval Forces (COMAR) Indochina, there were COMAR Tonkin and COMAR Mekong, the latter in Cochin-China. Subordinate COMARs reached down to the smallest station, COMAR Phat Diem being a lieutenant (junior grade) commanding two or sometimes three naval craft and several sampans.

Regional commands for offshore surveillance were established under Commander Naval Division, Far East. These were SURMAR (an acronym for *Surveillance Maritime*) Tonkin, covering the sector from the Chinese border south to 18° north, and SURMAR Annam, which controlled the area extending from 18° north to 10°30′ north to the Thailand border.[1]

Perhaps a third of FNEO thus constituted in effect what the French out there sometimes called the "white navy." The other good two-thirds certainly belonged to the "khaki navy," which operated the numerous smaller amphibious ships and craft in the Mekong and Red River deltas. In U.S. naval terms, there is a parallel distinction between the "brown water" (riverine) and "white water" (estuarine and coastal) navy on the one hand, and the "blue water" navy on the other.

The word in the "white navy" was that Indochina was a country of lotus-eaters, where young officers would lose themselves and forget everything. They would not get the benefit of fleet life, which alone formed good officers. If they were assigned to the amphibious forces, they would become deformed, forgetting the excellent precepts acquired at the naval academy and replacing them with unmentionable bad habits.

Indochina at this period effectively received all of the graduates of the naval academy, except for those who volunteered for flight training.

Arriving at Saigon, the newly assigned ensigns were divided between the "white navy" and the "khaki navy" (the southern Amphibious Force and the Northern Amphibious Force).[2]

SURVEILLANCE

SURMAR absorbed a good number of ships of the white navy. One cruiser, seven corvettes, six minesweepers, two escort ships, three launches, and two squadrons of naval observation aircraft had the formidable task of patrolling a coastline measuring approximately 1,500 nautical miles in length, an assignment that obviously could not be completely fulfilled with available ships and craft.

Nevertheless, the French navy reportedly achieved considerable success. Between 1,200 and 1,800 suspicious junks and sampans were hailed each quarter. Intelligence assessments indicated that, by 1950, Viet Minh infiltration by sea along the coast had been drastically reduced and perhaps eliminated in certain areas.

Even without the problem of weather, the French navy faced difficult problems in its maritime surveillance campaign. The legitimate activities of Vietnamese fishing and other small craft provided natural camouflage for the enemy's efforts to move men, arms, and supplies within Indochina, or to introduce these sinews of war from China. A French naval officer once related how, from a single point off the Annamese coast, he counted more than 500 small craft whose sails appeared to touch each other, giving the appearance of a white sea. The formidable problem, in these circumstances, was to identify which, if any, of the myriad small craft were operating in the service of Ho Chi Minh.

The task of interdiction was further complicated by effective Viet Minh control of a number of islands in the Gulf of Siam, coastal regions near Vinh in Tonkin, between Tourane and Nha Trang in Annam, and Cape Camau in Cochin-China. Geographic factors compounded the problem, since the heavily indented coastline of much of Indochina offered numerous hiding places.

During the northeast monsoon season from October through March, the French considered the seas off the northern part of Indochina too rough to allow extensive waterborne traffic. During that time naval leaders diverted their major attention to southern waters. When favorable weather returned to the north, the French shifted back the bulk of their patrol units.[3]

U.S. MILITARY AID

Fifteen million dollars in immediate, direct U.S. aid was now on the way. About $2 million was programmed for 12 LCVPs (landing craft, vehicle, personnel) and six LSSLs (landing ships, support, large), and about $6 million for 40 naval aircraft. French carrier *Dixmude* hurriedly loaded F6F Hellcat fighters and SB2C Helldiver bombers for delivery to Indochina. More LCVPs and LSSLs as well as other small craft and equipment were soon to be en route.[4]

Even though U.S. military aid directly identifiable as being for the Indochina war had until 1950 been denied, the French navy had indeed utilized U.S. materiel provided under the 1944 lend-lease program. Included in this category were escort carrier *Dixmude* (via the British) herself, three destroyer escorts (*Somali*, *Sénégalais*, and *Algérien*), at least four minesweepers, two coastal oilers, and several small escorts. These ships could now be refitted and updated.

Otherwise, up to this time, most outside help had come through receipt of a minor amount of German war booty, and through the sympathetic, friendly British.

Through other programs, France acquired 15,800-ton U.S.-built light carriers *La Fayette* and sister *Bois Belleau* (623 feet long, 32 knots, 26 aircraft) in 1951 and 1953, respectively. These were both to show up in Indochina before the end.

French LST *Rance*, escorting the six LSSLs and herself carrying the first shipment of LCVPs, reached Saigon late in November. The long-awaited aid was put right to work. At long last—thanks in no small part to the North Korean attack south into South Korea in June 1950—U.S. aid was flowing to the hard-fighting French Indochina naval forces. It proved to be none too soon, nor too much.

Naval aid from the United States now permitted the French to form two new *dinassauts*. Two continued to operate in the Mekong delta, and the two new *dinassauts* reinforced the four already operating in Tonkin. They could easily have used two more.

Prior to receipt of U.S. aid, the French navy in Indochina would have lacked sufficient strength to accomplish their tasks. Quite simply, there were just not enough of them to do the job.

Moreover, many of the riverine units, having operated at maximum effort for many years, were burned out. A lot of their original equipment was worn, much of it no longer truly serviceable. Some had been damaged beyond proper repair.

At this point came a navy-related event highly interesting in itself, but with even more interesting side aspects. The navy was having some second thoughts about riverine war. It was somewhat uneasy about being sucked into the twisted creeks and fetid swamps, and felt it was losing its soul (see Appendix A).

MON CAY (OPERATION *SAINT SYLVESTRE*)

By the time U.S. military aid had in the summer and fall of 1950 finally begun to arrive, however, the French Union situation ashore had become extremely precarious. Cao Bang and Langson—on the far northern border, in the hills, guarding the historic passes into China—had had to be abandoned. What had been a trickle of communist support coming across the border was becoming a flood.

Only the last of these historic forts—Mon Cay, on the coast—was still in French hands. Its so far successful defense rested primarily on the fact that here at least sea power could be fully and steadily brought to bear in support of the forces ashore.

By default, perhaps, no major army commands being at the moment available, it was the navy that now was charged with insuring that the tricolor continued to fly over this fortress city.

Therein lies a story. It had been the navy, early on, that almost alone had restored law and order to the far south. It was the service that really cleaned up the Mekong delta. But once the navy had put the expeditionary corps ashore in Haiphong, it had more and more reverted to a supporting role in what in the north was essentially a land war. The defense of Mon Cay gave it an opportunity to again play a major operational role, other than with *dinassauts*. It did.

On October 30th in Hanoi, at a meeting of the council of Defense, General Alessandri suggested that in face of the mounting threat Mon Cay and Hongay should both be evacuated. The troops thus released could help strengthen those in the delta proper.

Vice Admiral Paul-Ange-Philippe Ortoli (then Commander FNEO) objected strongly, holding that the loss of Mon Cay would seriously weaken the French position in the Tonkin Gulf. Ortoli was accordingly given the responsibility of holding the fortress port.

Deploying all available naval forces to the north, Admiral Ortoli managed to sufficiently reinforce the small garrison. By December 30th, naval commandos, Foreign Legionnaires, and local levees had all been scraped up and added to the defense. Supplied by sea and amply supported by naval gunfire—particularly the guns of cruiser *Duguay-Trouin*—the last of the old historic French border positions held on. Ortoli must have welcomed the chance to show what the navy could do.

The Viet offensive—begun here on December 26—had by early January 1951 run itself out.

As a result, Mon Cay, along with the coal mines at Campha

just to the south, remained securely in French hands until the armistice.

THE VIET DRIVE ON THE DELTA (NINH BINH)

Now in control of land lines of communication from China, fully organized, supplied, and trained, Giap prepared his army for a major—even final—drive down from the mountains into the Red River delta to take Hanoi. The French ability to repulse this offensive hinged essentially on their control and use of the extensive delta waterways and on naval support of land operations. As always, here.

Their preparations complete, in mid-January 1951, the Viet Minh confidently launched their long-awaited all-out assault. The Viets, 40,000 strong, stormed the French lines in the Vinh Yen area, 40 miles northwest of Hanoi, at an important road junction in the fringes of the delta. Here they deployed 30 to 40 battalions for a daylight battle in open country for the first time. Viet troops achieved tactical surprise, but Giap had underestimated the French ability, aided by inland naval power, to react.

Badly outnumbered, three to one, de Lattre took Ortoli's carefully calculated risk; he stripped the garrisons of South Vietnam. Gathering together in this way 11 battalions of reinforcements, he flew them to Vinh Yen in a ramshackle armada of military and civilian aircraft. General Charles Chanson was left to defend the south with only a handful of regulars and native auxiliaries. Then, personally, de Lattre cut the Viet Minh assault to pieces, skillfully supporting his troops with napalm and artillery.

One-third of the troops arrived in the vicinity of Vinh Yen in naval convoys that had steamed up the river past Hanoi. By the time the battle ended on January 17th, the Viets reportedly had lost 6,000 men.

Two months later, on March 23rd, Giap tried again. This time the assault was aimed at Mao Khe, on the northern border of the delta, about 20 miles northwest of Haiphong and astride the coastal road from China. After three days of fighting, the Viet Minh had overwhelmed all but one of the French outposts guarding the city. At that crucial point, the massing rebels were dispersed by gunfire from *Duguay-Trouin*, *Chevreuil*, *Savorgnan de Brazza*, and two landing support ships (LSSL-4 and LSSL-6) steaming on the Da Bach River just north of the city. Troops, including navy commandos and a paratroop battalion, reinforced the 400 defenders of Mao Khe. Two days later the Viet Minh thrust was finally repulsed.

Despite heavy losses at Vinh Yen and Mao Khe, Giap attempted once more to breach the delta defenses. This time he approached from the south. At least 40,000 Viet Minh regulars attacked French lines along the Day River. The battle began on the night of May 28–29, 1951, with an assault on Ninh Binh, where the determined resistance of a French navy commando unit slowed the enemy advance. The next day *Dinassaut* 3 sailed for Ninh Binh from Man Dinh with a convoy of one LCT, four LCMs, three LCVs (landing craft, vehicle), and several LCVPs, carrying reinforcements to the besieged town. Twelve kilometers from Ninh Binh, the Viet Minh sprang an ambush. After a brisk engagement, the *dinassaut* made its way to Ninh Binh. Some 20,000 reinforcements were rushed into the area by river, road, and air.

OPERATION *FOUDRE*

De Lattre counterattacked at once. On May 30th, *Dinassaut* 3, together with two temporary *dinassauts* organized for the emergency, provided mobility and naval gunfire support. The battle climaxed on June 4th and 5th with the fight for Yen Cu Ha, a few miles south of Ninh Binh. An LSSL arrived just as the enemy entered the town. After a round from the ship's 76-mm gun hit the watchtower where the enemy centered his defenses, Viet Minh resistance crumbled and the French attack carried the post. Fifty-five enemy soldiers trapped in the tower surrendered to the advancing French.

The key to victory in this campaign was control of the Day River by French naval forces. Deploying as many as 45 boats in the operation, river patrols severed Viet lines of communication. Fresh troops brought into the area then overwhelmed the isolated Viet forces. By June 18th, the battles for the delta were over. When the heavy rains began, bringing major military operations to a halt until the fall, Giap had taken a severe beating. The shattered remains of his army retreated to limestone hills to the west.[5]

Led by General de Lattre, strengthened by American aid, and fighting in areas where naval forces could operate, the French had won the winter and spring campaigns of 1951 in Tonkin. Viet Minh regular forces had suffered serious losses and would need time to recuperate.

THE "DE LATTRE PLAN"

From these actions in the north, the famous "de Lattre Plan" began to take form. As is usual with such things, it was built partly on what was already there, partly on what was forced on him by the enemy, and partly on inspired logic.

As Giap's main forces retired to rebuild their badly battered units, de Lattre carried out mopping-up operations within the Red River delta and went ahead with plans to organize mobile defenses along the line enclosing the Red River delta and the coastal region north to the Chinese border. The navy's task was—as usual—to patrol the waterways in the area, keeping them open.

De Lattre had already begun to withdraw the many scattered, small, isolated posts that were constantly falling, being retaken, and falling again, with little advantage to anyone, and to consolidate his forces. Most of the troops were left in the delta, while the others concentrated in hedgehogs through the rest of the country that could be quickly reinforced by air. The rebels were forced to attack the delta in order to obtain food. When they came, de

Lattre's forces were in positions of strength from which they could beat them off.

Behind the front the general organized as reserves light armored groups so placed that one of them could reinforce any point on the perimeter of the delta within 45 minutes. When the French felt strong enough, they pushed out from the delta and made limited counterattacks. In this way the Viets were being worn out in a calculated campaign of attrition.

SURVEILLANCE

By far, the easiest way for the Viet Minh to deliver supplies to depots or base areas in the middle and southern sections of Vietnam was still by sea. To effect such deliveries from China and northern Vietnam, they relied on stealth. Hiding in the numerous inlets and bays along the coast or mingling with the myriad fishing junks or sampans, the Viets were difficult to detect. Even with the new ships and craft received from the United States, the French Navy still lacked the necessary ships and crews needed to fully patrol the entire coast or to inspect all the traffic.

As a result, arms and ammunition, rice, salt, and sugar were continually being brought down and moved about.

To accomplish this, the communists used a number of tactics to avoid French patrols. Rebel junks would sometimes put out from Hainan Island and head south, well offshore, blending in with the normal traffic. Often timing their arrival for a moonless night, the junks would move in to the coast at a point near a Viet base and unload their critical cargo. At other times, the Viets transported supplies from point to point along the coast. Moving only at night, and close inshore, the tiny flotillas often sent out a reconnaissance junk disguised as a fishing boat. If this boat spotted a French patrol, the others beached until the danger had passed.

In attempting to choke off the supplies coming in by sea, the French used an average of fifteen to twenty ships, plus reconnaissance aircraft of the naval air arm, to search for suspicious contacts. Lacking modern radar on their patrol ships, the French often used ambush tactics, whereby they anchored near heavily traveled infiltration routes in hopes of catching Red craft moving at night.

In addition to their patrol efforts, the French raided such Viet Minh coastal bases as they could uncover. To go back, in one amphibious raid, Operation *Pirate*, on August 30, 1951, they assaulted a communist base that had been established on Cu Lao Re, an island off the central coast north of Quang Ngai. Two ex-German seaplane tenders, *Commandant Robert Giraud* and *Marcel le Bihan*, already equipped with heavy duty booms, carried LCVPs in the spaces previously assigned to aircraft. Escort *La Capricieuse* accompanied them.

Supported by gunfire from the ships, two naval commando companies landed over the beach. Together with army paratroopers, who arrived an hour later, the commandos cleared the island. Supplies for a permanent outpost were delivered by an LCT the next day. Henceforth, rather than serve as a transshipment point for war materials to communists on the coast, Cu Lao Re would function as a base to cut off the flow of such supplies along the coast.

By the same token, while the Viets lost a valuable observation post, the French gained one. From here, they could easily monitor activity on the central coast, and with a minimum of effort.

To increase the effectiveness of their maritime patrol efforts, FNEO now set up a third subordinate command, Commander Naval Aviation, under COMAR Indochina. It was assigned land-based squadrons of Sea Otter observation aircraft and PBY-6 Catalina amphibian patrol planes, based near Saigon at Cat Lai and Tan Son Nhut respectively. Catalinas also were based near Haiphong at Cat Bi. Although used primarily for observation and coastal surveillance missions, the naval air units flew under the operational control of the Air Force commander in Indochina.

OPERATIONS IN THE 1951 FALL COUNTEROFFENSIVES

General de Lattre planned to launch his own offensive that fall. The objective of Operation *Lotus* was to gain control of the Black River between Hoa Binh and the point where its waters joined those of the Red River on the way to the sea. If successful, *Lotus* would cut supply routes from the north to the Viet Minh forces in the southern regions of Tonkin.

Admiral Ortoli's ability to support further operations ashore gained a new dimension when light aircraft carrier *Arromanches* and her 44 aircraft (F6F and SB2C) arrived off Indochina in September 1951 after a 20-month absence. During a seven-month deployment she launched over 1,400 sorties in a wide variety of missions, including bombing runs against Viet Minh bases, close air support, convoy escort, and air reconnaissance. With the carrier's ability to range along the coast, tactical naval air could be concentrated where needed. *Arromanches*'s operations were all the more notable since the period of her cruise, coinciding with the northeast monsoon, was unfavorable for close support and visual bombing in the north, and it was there that the main targets—the Viet army forces—were located.

The success of de Lattre's fall campaign would depend in large measure on riverine operations and on the transportation of troops and supplies by water, sustaining the extended French army. French naval officers participating in planning for the operation pointed out the vulnerability of river communications to ambush along the Black River near Hoa Binh, but their warnings went unheeded.

HOA BINH

In preparation for *Lotus*, the French formed a temporary *dinassaut* of eight LCMs and four patrol craft and established a river command post at Trung Ha. Then, on November 14, 1951, three French paratroop battalions occupied Hoa Binh. Additional troops from the delta approached the city along Route 6. Others were transported in landing craft up the Black River, winding their way through the delta to Lang Tu Vu, at the base of the foothills of the Annamese mountain chain and then to Hoa Binh. Success! Or so it seemed.

Giap's obvious riposte was to cut the river communications line. He focused his main attacks carefully, against the river line at a point where the highlands on either side provided ideal cover for the Viet Minh, just as naval officers had feared. Even after Lang Tu Vu fell to Giap's by now fully aroused and massed Viet communists, the French continued to push river convoys through to Hoa Binh in the face of ever-mounting casualties from ambushes. Then on January 12, 1952, the Viet Minh ambushed a convoy south of Notre Dame Rock. In the face of murderous fire, the escorts raked the banks with their machine guns. In former engagements, their fire had enabled convoys to make their way through ambushes, but this time intense Viet Minh firepower forced the units to turn back. An LSSL and four patrol boats were sunk. Further efforts to force convoys up the river were abandoned.

Outnumbered and inferior in firepower, more and more ambushes intercepted supplies coming by land from the delta along Route 6. General Raoul Salan ("The Mandarin"), who had relieved the cancer-stricken de Lattre of his duties as commander in January 1952, became convinced that the value of controlling Hoa Binh was not worth the cost. By February 24th he had withdrawn his forces. Two LCMs, trapped upriver by low water, were sunk during the withdrawal, one by Viet fire and the other by its own crew to keep it from falling into enemy hands.[6]

IN MEMORIUM

Under de Lattre's command, strengthened by American aid and fighting in areas where the full impact of his naval support could be brought to bear, the French had turned the Indochina war around. For an historical moment or two, it had seemed that a respectable compromise solution to the political problem really might be won.

After de Lattre, in retrospect, it is clear that a certain fire went out of the French effort in Indochina. Support in Paris was waning, too. None of the subsequent commanders in chief enjoyed de Lattre's towering military prestige or his political support at home. As a result none had equal politico-military authority to carry out his ideas. None of those who came after him had his masterly grasp of the situation, or his brilliant generalship, or his courage, or his flair. He led!

De Lattre had returned to France in November and died in January. He was posthumously promoted to Marshal of France and buried in Les Invalides in Paris. He had lost his only son in the fighting at Phat Diem the previous year. De Lattre had been but a bright, short-lived meteor flashing across the sky in Indochina. After his departure, France's days were numbered.

The Indochina war was primarily a land war. Consequently, the navy overall played only a secondary role. It was ultimately the quality of the commander in chief—always an army general—that determined the fate of the French. Among the naval forces, it was the khaki navy which reflected that quality most directly. After "*le roi Jean*," all of the commanders appeared somehow smaller, more mediocre, than before.[7]

NOTES

1. Edwin B. Hooper, Dan C. Allard, and Oscar P. Fitzgerald, *The United States Navy and the Vietnam Conflict: The Setting of the Stage to 1959* (Washington, D.C.: Naval History Division, 1976), pp. 136–38.

2. Bernard Estival, *L'Enseigne dans le Delta* (Versailles: Editions les 7 Vents, 1989), pp. 13–14.

3. Hooper, Allard, and Fitzgerald, loc. cit.

4. Ibid., pp. 171–76, 178–79.

5. Jacques Mordal, *The Navy in Indochina* (Paris: Amiot-Dumont, 1953), pp. 266–70.

6. Hooper, Allard, and Fitzgerald, op. cit., pp. 188–89.

7. Estival, op. cit., pp. 19–20.

4

THE *DINASSAUTS*

THE MILITARY SETTING

At this point it might seem worthwhile to stop our historic progression and take a larger and more detailed look at how Jaubert's *dinassauts* had developed, their organization, and some of their tried-and-true assault and convoy tactics. By 1952, those tactics may be said to have reached their ultimate French form. Out of the *dinassauts*, subsequent South Vietnamese and U.S. river assault groups grew.

There had never before been anything quite like the *dinassauts*. There had indeed been shallow-draft river gunboats on the Mississippi. And on the Nile and the Shatt-al-Arab. Whatever troop elements found themselves actually involved in river operations—usually army units—ordinarily were carried up and down in separate conventional river passenger vessels. They were not specially organized, trained, or equipped for river combat from these craft.

Small French gunboats had worked the rivers of Indochina since the time of Garnier and Rivière. But they themselves could field only small landing parties, temporarily made up from the crews. Troop units were occasionally involved in their operations, but they were not organic to the ships and not specially trained in river combat. *Dinassauts* integrated both elements under one command and then gave them ramped, self-propelled landing craft. The operational results were dramatic: assault, patrol, transport, escort.

ORGANIZATION OF RIVER FORCES

Any too specific generalizing on *dinassaut* organization is bound to result in error. There were both permanent and temporary *dinassauts*. The exact composition of even the regular *dinassauts* varied. They were organized pragmatically at birth and continued in that vein until the end. Their composition over time reflected basic differences in geography of the various operational areas, and the requirements of specific tasks in hand.

We can identify, however, those elements common to most *dinassauts*. The river flotillas each contained an assortment of small craft, a base, a repair yard, river control posts, and for some coastal posts. Some of these facilities were so primitive as to be hardly recognizable as such.

Within this framework operated the *dinassauts* proper. They were the striking element. To them was added whatever was both necessary and available at the time. LSSLs, monitors, LCTs, and minesweepers fell among the latter class, sometimes quasi-permanently, sometimes only attached for a specific job.

It can be said, however, that specific *dinassauts* were made up of from 12 to 18 craft. See Table 1 for their generalized organization, including the types of ships and crafts involved and their individual functions within the units.[1] It should be remembered that Table 1 only represents almost an ideal organization, all elements of which were seldom seen at the same time.

Table 1
Dinassaut Organization (Basic)

function	type of ship or craft
command	one LSIL or LCM
fire support	one attached LSSL and/or two to four monitors
minesweeping	two to four attached LCM(M)s
transport	one or more LCTs or LCUs
assault	four or more LCVPs
patrol	armed launches or motor sampans
liaison	armed launches

Each *dinassaut* could land an organic commando force of reinforced company size or a stripped down infantry battalion. Their organic complement could reach as high as 800 officers and men.

Each *dinassaut* carried a powerful organic mix of weapons: 3-inch, 40-mm, 37-mm, 20-mm cannon; 50- and 30-caliber machine guns. Many added 81- and 120-mm mortars, providing organic high angle fire support.

As can be seen, Jaubert's Gressier barges had changed into a number of specialized military types, gradually procured over the years, bought, borrowed, or received as aid. Most were recognizable World War II amphibious models, from leftover British and American stock. Toward the end of the war, newer types (LCUs, for instance) began to arrive, however.

Some of these craft were more useful than others, appearing in the after-action reports again and again, some in large numbers. LSSLs (landing ships, support, large), LCMs (landing craft, mechanized), LCTs (landing craft, tank), and LCVPs (landing craft, vehicle, personnel) fall into that category.

SHIPS AND CRAFT

LSSLs were the capital ships of the riverine forces. They were some 160 feet long, their eight diesels giving them 14 knots. Armed with one 76-mm gun, four 40-mm and four 20-mm, two 81-mm mortars, and two machine guns, they boasted a 30- to 50-man crew. They maneuvered and were organized like true naval ships. As ships, they had official names (not just numbers) like *Arquebuse*, *Javeline*, and *Pertuisane*, ancient weapons all.

LSSLs like most other ships were organizationally independent of *dinassauts*. They were placed under the operational control of *dinassaut* commanders only for specific jobs, if and as needed. Otherwise they were under the direct orders of the amphibious force headquarters.

In the middle years, LSSLs themselves sometimes were sent to raid alone into enemy-held territory. If so, they would take on board an artillery forward observer, making heavy indirect fire support available on call. However, LSSLs lacked sufficient crew to make up a landing party truly large enough to fully follow up on their fire.

LSILs were their close cousins, LSSLs being in fact built on LSIL hulls. They were armed with 40- and 20-mm guns, but lacked the LSSL's 76-mm. In exchange, they provided interior spaces for command, control, and communications, and for up to 200 troops. They too had names.

LCTs came in both naval and civilian versions. One hundred twenty to 192 feet long, originally built for landing three medium tanks on enemy beaches, in Indochina they were generally used for carrying up to 200 tons of food, fuel, ammunition, or other general cargo in bulk. Four diesels gave them 12 knots. These had crews of up to 30. They developed into LSMs.

LSMs were a seagoing version of the LCTs, at the larger end

of the spectrum. They could carry five tanks. Diesels gave them, too, a speed of 12 knots. They carried crews of around 50.

The 56-foot LCMs—the ubiquitous LCMs—could each deliver a heavy tank or its equivalent (120 men or 30 tons of cargo) to a beach. They had crews of five or six, as a rule. A pair of diesels gave them speeds of up to nine knots; having three gave them ten knots. These were very versatile boats, being the largest deck-loaded on board a transport. Some of their hulls were converted into monitors or sweepers.

LCAs were 40-foot craft. Equipped with two engines, two heavy machine guns, and lightly armored, they were capable of carrying and landing a platoon (30 men). They might have a crew of eight.

Also mentioned from time to time were LSTs. LSTs were ocean tank carriers equipped with bow doors, operating shore to shore. The basic model was 327 feet long, displacing 1,625 tons, diesel powered like the rest of the amphibious family, capable of 11 knots. LSTs carried 140 troops and a crew of 80. They had little to do directly with *dinassaut* affairs, being more properly considered a part of the logistic train, operating coast-wise.

LCPs were 36-foot boats driven by a single diesel. They were designed to assault land troops but they could also handle up to four tons of cargo. They had three-man crews. These were an early design, soon phased out, the boats ending up as utility craft around bases and in ports.

LCVPs succeeded them. These were 36-foot boats also driven by a single diesel. They were also designed to assault land troops but they could in addition handle small vehicles such as jeeps. They also had three-man crews. Of these there were many, in use right up to the end.

Toward the end, the United States began furnishing a number of the newer LCUs. These 118-foot craft could carry three tanks or their cargo equivalent. Three diesels gave them speeds of up to ten knots. Almost landing ships, their crews ran to a dozen men. LCUs tended to replace both LSMs and LCTs, substituting for both.

All of these amphibious craft were of shallow draft. All of the *craft* had bow ramps. All except the LCVPs were built of welded steel. LCVPs were constructed of wood. All were diesel-powered.

Once landing craft arrived in Indochina from Singapore or Manila—or in the last years of the United States—they were taken in hand and three things done to them. In the early days, they had to be armed. Later, their armament had to be increased. They were to some extent armored. Insofar as possible, their habitability was improved. And those that had to be modified, were.

Most monitors were based on LCM hulls, armored and armed with a tank turret, a local improvisation of the delta navy yards. Riding low in the water, strongly protected, relatively powerfully armed, monitors provided *dinassauts* with an element of shock.

After close-in fire from bazookas, mortars, and machine guns, probably the greatest danger in the river war came from mines. Enemy river mines were fairly crude homemade bottom mines, their firing controlled by observation from the bank. They were exceedingly effective, nonetheless, in that they were sunk deep in the mud and almost defied sweeping.

To sweep them, the French converted a number of LCMs into LCM(M)s, giving them heavy wire drags, grapples, and chains with which to plow the mud.[2] This technique met with only partial success, but it was the best there was.

As the Viets gradually became aware of the importance of the waterways to the French, they resorted to any number of means to block their waterways. One of their more common methods was to sink a bamboo barricade into the bottom, forcing the *dinassauts* out of the middle closer in toward one shore or the other, where they were more easily ambushed. Or mined. The Viets scuttled sampans full of rocks and felled trees, for the same purpose.

By this time, the riverine forces were supported by a number of light observation aircraft known as "crickets." These planes operated over the front and flanks of a convoy and, flying at low speeds and low altitudes, provided good information on what was ahead. These crickets were able at times to locate even the camouflaged fire control points used to fire the Viet mines.

Crickets in trouble were easily salvageable. They could land almost anywhere on dikes or dry rice paddies. Damaged planes could be loaded on an LCT. They were useful additions to the team, always welcomed by the *dinassaut* crews.

Like the LSSLs, the monitors, sweepers, and crickets were organized into independent units, starting with sections of two. They were also assigned and shifted about as needed.

PERSONNEL

By now, Amphibious Forces Indochina had a Group North and a Group South. In the north, river assault groups—the basic river units—were now permanently stationed at such places as Haiphong, Hanoi, Nam Dinh, Ninh Giang, Sept Pagodes, and elsewhere. In the south, they were stationed at My Tho, Can Tho, and Cape St. Jacques. Detached groups were also located at Pnom-Penh in Cambodia and at Vientiane in Laos.

The commanding officers of these river assault groups—by 1952, all commanders in rank—now had acquired specific sector responsibilities, had established fixed control posts, had acquired good detailed knowledge of their assigned areas, and were at high levels of effectiveness. They all had established fixed command posts ashore, and were local COMARs. To them were assigned or attached the necessary troops, river craft, and planes, assuring their command and support, and the successful accomplishment of their tasks.

Temporary *dinassauts* were formed from time to time for specific purposes. Some of these became quasi-permanent. Their organization was usually somewhat simpler than that of the regular units, tailored to their task, their commanders often more junior.

One typical *dinassaut* (river assault group 3, stationed at Nam Dinh) occupied a villa and its outbuildings situated on the bank of a river (the Nam Dinh Giang), near their "beaching." There had always to be a hard "beach" as well as shelter. There its ships and craft were moored, worked on side by side, bows firmly pushed into the bank, rear held out across the current by a long cable leading to a stern anchor.

For the navy in Indochina, tours of duty were officially of two lengths: for the white navy, two years; for the khaki, 18 months. Reliefs, however, generally ran three or four months late. Tours were repeatable by agreement of all parties.

Life in the khaki navy was never plush. The spartan, cramped landing *ships* were large enough to be lived on, and their crews did so. The smaller landing *craft* were not; their crews only berthed on board during times on the river, living in the well, open to the sky. They slept in hammocks, under mosquito nets and ponchos. Otherwise, they berthed ashore in a variety of billets, some marginally better than others. Still, there was a hard core of adventurers who kept coming back.

For these adventurers, fighting was their business. Many found Indochina fascinating, in any case. Still others discovered the relative independence an early combat command gave them, and were proud.

Off-duty conversation among the officers revolved around the rivers. In the north there were stories of convoys on the Nam Dinh Giang, of ambushes on the Day, of mines at Pass 37, of bazookas in the limestone rocks, of the Catholics of Bui Chu, of the currents that reversed at Kilometer 24, of the shifting sandbars of Cua Balat, of the respective merits of 40-mm and 20-mm guns, of the quality of the water at the Nam Dinh cotton mill. There was not much else.

Dinassaut bases—exposed and alone—were highly vulnerable to guerrilla attack. Base defense proved a serious problem, and remained so. Toward the end, they were under what amounted to permanent siege. Still, entertainment was found.

In 1953, Cyclone Betty hit the north hard, passing over COM-AR Phat Diem's small base. A week later Naval Headquarters in Hanoi received an impressive list of surveyed lost items, all simply laid to "Cyclone Betty." Government property, all of it.

Hanoi considered this a little summary and requested Phat Diem to be so good as to furnish it with sufficient detail. COMAR Phat Diem—a lieutenant (junior grade), please remember—felt that his word was in question. He responded with a report 40 pages long, in six copies, relating the passage of the depression, accompanied by barometric, anemometric, and rain gauge readings, completed by eyewitness statements. His report naturally made the tour of the north, giving at the same time satisfaction to headquarters, which could never overlook its rights.

One favorite book that went the rounds of the deltas was called *Cahiers de Louis, Adhémar, Timothée le Golif dit Borgnefesse, Capitaine de la Flibuste, 1952*, published by Grasset in Paris (1952). The title alone would make it interesting during dull times, war being weeks of sheer boredom punctuated by moments of absolute terror.[3]

COMBAT OPERATIONS

A *dinassaut* generally deployed for approach movement in column, led by one or more LCM monitors, followed by an open group of minesweepers (three two-boat sections and a spare). At a short interval behind the lead group would follow an LSSL or armed LCT fire support ship, followed in turn by the transport element and the assault element. When there was but one support ship, it was the command ship; when there were two, the command ship was the rear one. Sometimes the transport craft moved in a double column, lashed together in pairs.

Typically, delta rivers wound for miles through the flatlands, passing silent villages and small blockhouses. The rivers were edged with mangrove or other dense greenery, sometimes with wide sandbanks, mud flats, and barricades of bamboo placed here and there across the main channel. Even the friendly blockhouses disappeared after the first few miles, to be replaced by a feeling of menace.

As the *dinassaut* thrummed upstream into enemy country, the riverbanks, at first thronged with cheering locals, would fall empty and silent. Along the rivers where no one was to be seen, by day a succession of gaily colored kites slowly rose into the air, marking the force's progress. By night, drums marked its passage. It is difficult to convey the impression of hostility left on the crews.[4]

In an actual assault, the leading and clearing group was followed at 750 meters by the shock group: a command vessel, one or more fire support ships to lay a prelanding bombardment, and landing craft carrying the assault troops. The remainder of the force trailed at a distance of 1,000 to 1,500 meters. Once a landing site was secured, these too would beach and unload.

During the landing and until the *dinassaut* was withdrawn, the force afloat provided fire support, protected the flanks of the "beaching," and patrolled up and down the river. Some craft were used for logistic (supply, medical evacuation, and other noncombat) support, and the larger ships sometimes served as command posts for the troop units.[5]

On occasion, the *dinassauts* raided along the borders of controlled delta territory. For several days a river assault group would comb an area, interrogating the villagers (who of course had seen nothing), looking for arms caches and occasionally finding them (seizing a few arms and almost always several documents, as the Viets were great producers of paper). The *dinassaut* would then pull out, blowing a few bridges and one or two fortified buildings, bringing a few suspects out with it as it went.[6]

One standard tactic was repeated again and again. Troops—organic naval infantry or, for larger operations, army units—would be landed by the *dinassauts* across the base of a peninsula or river bend, and the craft then stationed in blocking positions around the watersides. The troops would then drive the rebels against the river, to be killed or captured by the French.

Portions of the river could always be blocked off, preventing the enemy's crossing or otherwise using it. One could, for this purpose, anchor all one's craft in the middle of the channel or one could beach them all along the reach, spaced at such a distance that any attempt to cross would be noticed by at least one among them. Either had the advantage of discretion, but aside from the fact that both required numbers of craft, they ran the risk of seeing the enemy force a passage after having neutralized any one craft before the others had an opportunity to intervene.

The alternative tactic consisted in remaining continually under way, patrolling the reach frequently enough to prevent any crossing between the intervals. In this case, each craft patrolled only a portion of the reach. Of course, the craft could not hide their presence; the engine noise saw to that. But moving they were less vulnerable and could rapidly be concentrated in case of need.[7]

Returning from a raid was for a *dinassaut* like running a gauntlet. Returning could be as costly as getting there, or even more so. On the way in, the force would pass silent villages, noting the prepared mortar and machine gun positions that were waiting for their return. Objective accomplished, a *dinassaut* would regroup and head back out, manning every gun.

At an ambush, general fire would explode on both sides, the Viets pouring short-range bazooka and machine gun fire down from high banks on either side or from carefully camouflaged bunkers deep in the woods. A *dinassaut* might have to run such a murderous gauntlet as much as seven kilometers long and fight off the equivalent of an entire enemy battalion.[8]

In the early days, a *dinassaut* could almost always run such an ambush successfully. Using their immensely superior firepower, the khaki sailors would lay a deadly "fireball" over the enemy, smothering his fire. Some casualties were inevitable, in any case.

Toward the end, a *dinassaut* had to be considerably stronger than before just to run a Viet ambush. The enemy had better weapons, and there were more of them. The guerrillas became more skilled at conducting their ambushes, too.

The *dinassauts* responded by increasing the size of the raiding forces and by adding to the amount of armor on their ships and craft. Each side kept escalating the problem, presenting a miniversion of the classical armor versus firepower battle.

CONVOYS

French Union forces in the delta depended by 1952 more than ever on lines of communication based on the inland waterways. Truck convoys were held up by blown roads. Even strong truck convoys took prohibitive losses from ambushes and mines. For the French, control of the rivers had become essential.

A typical river convoy might consist of an LSSL, a section of monitors, two sections of LCM(M)s, all for escort, and the convoy proper, the supply LCTs. As the convoy set its speed by that of the slowest craft, it usually moved at the river standard of seemingly four or five kilometers an hour.

In the Tonkin delta, supply convoys were thus made up primarily of LCTs—both military and civilian. LCTs moved not only anything that rolled, but practically anything of bulk—boxes of rations, rolls of barbed wire, cases of ammunition, cases of beer, bags of cement, bundles of steel rods, boxes of batteries. Both types of LCTs were themselves armed, sometimes powerfully.

In Tonkin, naval LCTs were generally commanded by lieutenants (junior grade) or limited duty officers of similar rank. Respecting tradition, the senior officer in charge of the escorted LCTs was always given the courtesy title of "commodore."[9]

During night movements, all ships and craft sailed entirely blacked out. This was less for secrecy—the noise of their engines precluded that—than to present the Viets along the banks a more difficult target. Craft would move in long columns, as much to be sure of remaining in the channel as for mutual support. They would be led by the sweepers, covered by an LSSL or monitor.

Crews were kept at action stations at all times while under way. The gun ships would often simply hose down every likely enemy ambush spot as they went, using their multiple 40- and 20-mm and 50-calibers. This at least forced the Viets to keep their heads down and sometimes even drove them off. Response to enemy fire had to be instant and overwhelming, and was.

As they went, supply convoys serviced the isolated small army posts along their route. They made sure everything was all right, exchanging messages. They picked up requisitions and delivered completed orders. They provided emergency communications and medical evacuation as needed.

Working minesweepers were easy to spot. Pulling heavy drags, their engines had to run at full power. When under strain, their engines spewed volumes of white smoke.[10]

Minesweeping grapples often caught on the bottom, sometimes on a rock but more often on a wrecked sampan or a submerged tree stump. When this happened, the whole convoy had to stop while the sweepers cleared their drags, then repaired and restreamed their gear.

Navigation in the deltas was always a problem. It consisted entirely of pilotage, dead reckoning, and intuition. Buoyage had always been somewhat summary and sparse, but the Viets had removed most of the marks and moved many of the others. In any case, charts tended to be a half century old, only partially brought up to date. At night, craft had to cope with the ever-present mists. By day, there was rain and fog. There were twice-daily tides.

Lacking anything else, craft were routinely piloted by reference to corners of dikes, isolated trees, bell towers, pagodas, banana groves, bamboo clusters, steps along the riverbank. There was the rule that channels did not follow the middle of the river, but generally ran on the concave side of a turn, sand and mud bars being found on the convex side. A long bamboo sounding pole was an essential piece of gear.

By now, the French navy had committed more than 10,000 officers and men to the delta wars. The tiny new Vietnamese navy—under French command and tutelage—added 1,500 more.

CRESCENDO

But by 1952, the enemy—always ready to harry passing French river traffic—had begun systematically to attempt to bring it to a halt. The Viets had up to then paid it sporadic attention, but the increasing dependence of the French on their rivers and canals had finally caught their eye. This brought about a major escalation of the communist effort. Isolated LCTs sailing unescorted anywhere in the delta risked being sunk. With craft moving—sometimes against the current—at four or five kilometers an hour, the communists could hardly miss.

"Heavy" convoys became more and more the rule. If convoys were strong enough, the Viets would generally let them pass. But no more LCTs ran without sufficient escort. Lone LSSLs carried out fewer and fewer raids behind communist lines. At no time were convoys closed down, it should be noted. *That* would have guaranteed disaster.

In the delta, artillery support had always been somewhat difficult to arrange. Lacking firm ground on which to site their guns, artillery had often to be based on scows, moored to a bank. Artillery had its fire direction center there, fired from the scows, lived on them, and stored its ammunition there.

The artillery scows could and would be towed to new firing positions by sections, leapfrogging each other. This echeloning theoretically made at least some on-call fire available at all times to all moving units likely to need it. Such was not always the case.

Air support was in some ways simpler to arrange, not being range-limited if weather allowed. Weather, however, was not always flyable, either over the target, over the field, or both (see Appendix C).

The navy continued to conduct operations in the delta against infiltrating guerrilla units, as well as to strike the enemy in his bases and to escort convoys. The Viets responded with mining and ambushes.

Mining incidents averaged only perhaps one a month until near the end of 1953, a statistic only partially explained by the fact that the rebels needed the waterways, too. The Viets then further stepped up their efforts. LSIL 9030 was sunk south of Haiphong in January 1954, and mining incidents involving smaller craft occurred every few days (see Table 2).

Table 2
Selected River Ambushes (January 15–February 16, 1954)

Date	Place	Type Craft	Comments
Jan. 15	Nam Dinh Giang	LCT 9063 and barge convoy LCM	1 barge sunk; 4 Navy wounded; 1 Army killed
Jan. 22	Song Thai Binh	Dinassaut 1	Detected by "cricket," neutralized by artillery fire
Feb. 2	Day	LSSL LCM assault boats	1 boat burned; LSSL *Pertuisane* damaged; 4 Navy killed or missing; 2 wounded
Feb. 4	Upper Red River	LCM and *Mytho* Dinassaut 12	*Mytho* sunk; 1 Navy wounded
Feb. 9	Nam Dinh Giang	Dinassaut 3 LSSL	LSSL *Arquebuse* and 2 LCMs damaged; 3 Navy killed; 15 Navy wounded
Feb. 14	Middle Red River (Hung Yen)	Dinassaut 12	LCT 9047 damaged; 1 Army killed; 1 Army wounded; 4 Navy killed
Feb. 16	Nam Dinh Giang	Dinassaut 13	LCT 9033 damaged; 1 boat sunk; 1 LCM damaged; 1 killed; 7 wounded

In each of these ambushes, the French craft were hit primarily by a combination of bazooka and automatic weapons fire.

Source: Robert McClintock. "The River War in Indochina," U.S. Naval Institute *Proceedings* (December, 1954), p. 1308. Copyright U.S. Naval Institute, 1954. With permission.

Sweeping of the larger waterways by small tugs and of the shallower creeks and canals by LCM(M)s eventually brought the mine threat substantially—never completely—under control.

The ambushes were another problem. One day, the Viets attacked a French convoy near Hung Yen, between Nam Dinh and Hanoi. The convoy, on alert, responded as usual with all its weapons instantly. Then came something new for a convoy. LCMs carrying a small commando unit beached directly on the enemy positions, landing their commandos. Surprised in their emplacements, expecting to defend against machine gun and artillery fire, not commandos assaulting from flanks and rear, the Viets were overrun. They took heavy losses without inflicting any damage at all.[11]

At the end, convoys had to be escorted by *two* LSSLs as well as by two to four monitors. While slow, every convoy was preceded by sweepers from beginning to end of the trip. But the main improvement was the inclusion on LCMs of a commando prepared to intervene onshore in case of ambush.

By the end, any kind of movement on the rivers had taken on more and more of the aspects of a roaring, rolling brawl.

What with patrols, ambushes, and the occasional more extended operation, life on the river passed very quickly.

Orders into the Haiphong base—for ship or craft modification, repair, refit, or just simple bottom cleaning—were always a welcome respite from the fighting. The restaurants and other amenities of traditional interest to seamen to be found in town were both plentiful and cheap. On one LSSL, both the commanding officer and his first lieutenant shared the same mistress. Being French and civilized, the watch bill was adjusted accordingly, and while in Haiphong carefully followed.

Always leading, always out in front, from the Siamese frontier to that of China, on the rivers and the thousand canals and streams of Cochin-China, Annam, Tonkin, the *dinassauts* earned their salt. Jaubert had not worked in vain.

NOTES

1. Richard M. Meyer, "The Ground-Sea Team in River Warfare," *Military Review* (September 1966). This article is the inspiration for Table 1, but the table is a composite assembled by the author from many sources.

2. *Jane's Fighting Ships*—an annual naval forces reference book—is the best reference on ships and craft of the period. U.S. publishers were the McGraw-Hill Book Company, New York.

3. Bernard Estival, *L'Enseigne dans le Delta* (Versailles: Editions Les 7 Vents, 1989), passim.

4. Maurice R. de Brossard, "Dinassaut," *La Revue Maritime* (January 1953).

5. Barry Gregory, *Vietnam Coastal and Riverine Forces Handbook* (Wellingborough, England: Patrick Stephens, 1988), p. 98.

6. Estival, op. cit., p. 49.

7. Ibid., p. 66.

8. de Brossard, loc. cit.

9. Estival, op. cit., pp. 127–30.

10. Ibid., pp. 158–59.

11. Ibid., p. 159.

1. **France's Fast Battleship *Richelieu***
   Courtesy U.S. Naval Institute

2. France's Light Aircraft Carrier *La Fayette*
   Official U.S. Navy Photograph

3. **Troops Landing at Van Fong Bay**
Official U.S. Navy Photograph

4. Craft Approaching Ninh Binh
   Official U.S. Navy Photograph

5. French Ex-U.S. LSSL
   Courtesy U.S. Naval Institute

6. **French Ex-U.S. LSIL**
Courtesy U.S. Naval Institute

7. **French Ex-U.S. LSM**
Courtesy U.S. Naval Institute

8. **U.S. LCT(6)**
Courtesy U.S. Naval Institute

9. **U.S. LCM**
Courtesy U.S. Naval Institute

10. **French Ex-U.S. LCM**
Official U.S. Naval Photograph

11. **French River Assault Group**
    Official U.S. Navy Photograph

12. **French LCVPs**
Official U.S. Navy Photograph

13. **French Patrol Launches**
Official U.S. Navy Photograph

5

COLLAPSE?

As is often the case, the mounting military shortfall in Indochina was not immediately apparent to those on the scene. Two able generals in turn were to take over in Indochina—Salan and Navarre—before France at home had had its fill of this dirty little war.

In the middle of all this, the role of *Marine Indochine* not only continued, but grew. We shall follow all this to the end.

At this point—mid-1952—the situation in the Mekong delta was tolerable, although large portions of it were under the control of private armies rather than of the French or Bao Dai's armed forces.

In Annam, French control was still limited to the areas around Hué, Tourane, and Nha Trang. Although the coast road was open, it was dangerous to use, and most supplies moved by sea.

In Tonkin, the de Lattre line was absorbing the bulk of the available troops, leaving little of a maneuvering reserve. Giap was stronger than ever. But it was here in the north that the war could be won or lost, now. France searched for another general.

THE 1952 FALL OFFENSIVES

As fall approached, Giap launched his regular forces on another offensive. Early, the Viet Minh took the French by surprise and gained the initiative. An offensive had been expected, but not until later. Also, the direction of the offensive and its objective surprised the French, as operations commenced in the T'ai highlands of northwest Tonkin, an area remote from the sea. The Viet objective was the string of forts in the mountains between the Red and Black rivers. Giap concentrated his forces against Nghia Lo. After the fall of Nghia Lo on October 17, 1952, the small outposts on its flanks were either abandoned or overrun.

Thus began another winter of the most difficult kind of fighting. The French worked frantically to establish new defensive positions, but the initiative was again largely Ho's. By November the situation had developed into a three-front fight. The first was in the Red River valley, where 30,000 French were on the offensive. On the second, in the mountainous jungles of the Black River country, 10,000 Thais, Moroccans, and legionnaires fought three Viet divisions at Nasan. The third was in the Hanoi delta, where Giap had touched off a 40,000-man guerrilla attack to keep the French off balance.

As in the case of the communist attacks in the Viet Bac the previous year, the French army was not able to defend its position in jungled and mountainous regions remote from the sea, where it could not receive effective support from riverine forces. As a result of these victories and the failure of Operation *Lotus*, the Viets now controlled the inland lines of communication from Kwangsi and Yunnan.

Light carrier *Arromanches* returned to Indochinese waters that month for her third deployment. Through February 18, 1953, her aircraft flew 1,561 sorties, about one-third of the total number of French air force flights in North Vietnam. With the exception of a short period at the end of January and early February, when her aircraft hit targets in the central highlands of Vietnam, *Arromanches* operated in the Gulf of Tonkin off Haiphong.

After the carrier returned to France, her air group remained behind to operate from Cat Bi Airfield.

In order to disrupt the flow of supplies from China and the Viet base area in the Viet Bac, and at the same time relieve pressure on the T'ai region, General Salan decided to strike north of the Red River. Salan's operation there, a major effort, was dubbed "Operation *Lorraine*." It involved a French-Vietnamese tank-infantry force about 15,000 strong. On November 9th, in the biggest simultaneous movement of troops by air up until then, several thousand paratroopers joined with land and river units to seize Phudoan, 75 miles from Hanoi. The French then converged on the communist bases in the Yenbay–Phu Tho–Tuyenquang triangle.

Planning to use the Red, Clear, and Chay rivers as lines of communication, General Salan initially employed two LCIs, four monitors, five LCMs, and seven French river patrol boats from *Dinassauts* 3 and 12.

For several days prior to the operation, boats ferried a steady stream of supplies north from Hanoi to staging areas at Trung Ha on the Red River and Viet Tri on the Clear River. On October 29th, naval units assisted in bridging the Red River, as the task force moved out from Trung Ha heading for Phu Tho farther up the river. Just north of Phu Tho, at Ngoc Thap, on November 7th, the force linked up with a second column moving up from Viet Tri. The two columns continued northward to Phudoan (Doan Hung), a major communist supply base at the junction of the Clear and Chay rivers. As the forces marched overland toward Phudoan, river units advanced up the rivers.

In typical *dinassaut*-type actions, embarked Moroccan infantrymen and naval commandos were landed on the riverbanks to pursue the enemy. Patrols pushed to Phu Yen Binh on the Chay River, a point two-thirds of the way to Yunnan province from the mouth of the Red River.

The French-Vietnamese forces had temporarily cut routes to Chinese supply sources and had overrun substantial forward supply dumps. However, having failed to draw Giap's forces from the T'ai region and faced with the continuing danger of overextension, General Salan ordered a withdrawal of his forces on November 14th.

The French then turned back a Viet attack on Laos. For four months neither opponent mounted large-scale operations, although the countless small engagements throughout the country resulted in continuing casualties on both sides.[1]

NAVAL OPERATIONS ALONG THE COAST

Meanwhile, as they had once before—in 1946—the French used the mobility, surprise, and concentrated power of amphibious operations against the enemy in central Annam. Intelligence reported enemy buildups near the ancient city of Hué. Here, during the dry summer season in the north, the communists had deployed the Viet Minh 101st Regiment. Operation *Sauterelle* began on the night of August 24, 1952, along the coast north of the Perfume River. While landing forces from *Marcel Le Bihan* carried out two diversionary raids, three LSTs and three LCUs (landing craft, utility) along with LCMs and LCVPs, landed four army battalions and two navy commando companies. From his flagship, gunboat *Savorgnan de Brazza*, Rear Admiral Gabriel-Laurent Rebuffel, then assigned as commander of the coastal forces, directed the operation. Four escorts provided gunfire support.

The landings caught the Viet Minh by surprise, and four French army battalions, approaching from north and south, completed the encirclement. The troops met stiff resistance but the firepower of the ships offshore helped carry the day. On the afternoon of the 25th, *Savorgnan de Brazza*, with the help of an airborne spotter, leveled several rebel-held villages. During most of the night the gunboat fired star shells for illumination and conducted harassing fire. Escort *Commandant Duboc* also carried out nighttime missions in support of navy commandos, while *Chevreuil* evacuated 15 dead and 23 wounded army troopers to Tourane. Naval gunfire continued on the 26th and two navy PB4Y Privateers, based at Tourane, flew six bombing missions in support of the operation.

A typhoon delayed the reembarkation for two days, but on August 29th, three LSTs beached and took on troops, as escorts *Commandant Dominé* and *la Capricieuse* covered the withdrawal. Against a loss of 25 dead and 37 wounded, the French reported killing 107 and capturing 1,061 Viets.

In a follow-up operation, code-named *Caiman*, the surprise possible in an amphibious landing again was achieved. The target in this landing was the remnant of the same Viet Minh 101st Regiment that earlier threatened Hué. The amphibious forces were essentially those used in *Sauterelle*, but for *Caiman* the French army deployed ten battalions instead of four. The navy landed the troops at dawn on September 4, 1952, as ships lay offshore providing gunfire support throughout the day and night.

At 0030 on the 5th, the Viets mounted a desperate counter-attack, attempting to break through French troops toward the northwest. French North African troops and the naval commandos vigorously resisted and inflicted heavy losses on the enemy. The operation continued until the morning of September 7th when, despite unfavorable weather caused by another typhoon, the amphibious force again backloaded the landing force. *Caiman* realized results even more impressive than *Sauterelle*. The French reported 640 enemy killed, 1,400 captured, and large quantities of arms and ammunition seized.

QUINHON (OPERATION *TOULOUSE*)

With the new year, further major amphibious activity was resumed. Between January 29 and February 2, 1953, in the biggest naval operation of the war to date, French forces successfully raided Quinhon, rebel base on the coast. Participating were *Arromanches, Cdt. Robert Giraud,* four gunboats, and a mixed group of commandos and paras. Once ashore, the troops advanced five miles into the interior in a move to relieve pressure on Ankhe, then under heavy Viet attack. That done, they pulled out.

On April 18th, French forces landed to the north of Nha Trang, on the shore of Van Fong.

At this point, although the French had met with reverses in remote inland regions of Tonkin near the Chinese border, it should be recognized that they had not lost the war. They had at the same time, with the assistance of their navy, achieved notable military successes in the Red River delta and coastal regions since 1950. As a result, they had increased their control over the main centers of population, food, and industry. However, in view of the vast extent of Indochina's waterways and the lengthy coastline of Vietnam, the French navy's 12,000-man seagoing and riverine forces remained marginal at best.[2]

At the beginning of the monsoon season in 1953 in Indochina, as activity slowed, France took stock of the situation. Paris could not help but note that since the death of General de Lattre the overall situation had stagnated. The decision of the government of Premier René Mayer was to replace, on May 8, 1953, General Salan with cold, slim, neat, aggressive Lieutenant General Henri-Eugène Navarre.

NAVARRE

As commander in chief for Indochina, General Navarre developed an ambitious three-point strategic plan. First, he intended to regain the military initiative and to take the tactical offensive. Second, he decided to expand both French forces and the Vietnamese army, plus small additions from Laos and Cambodia, to an overall total of 500,000 men. This would enable the French Union to contest the control of every village and clearing, and still release mobile units to form a striking force for massive attacks on communist bases, concentrations, and supply lines. Third, he planned to speed up independence for Vietnam in order to gain full native support. Navarre's objective was to break the backbone of communist resistance through direct engagement of their regular forces. Should he be successful, the expanded native forces alone would be able to assume full responsibility for the defense of the country.

During the summer of 1953, Navarre broke the usual pattern of the monsoon with a continuous series of reconnaissance and combat patrols and harassing attacks. He launched a well-executed airborne assault on the communist base at Langson, 50 miles behind communist lines, in mid-July.

Next, Navarre destroyed a cluster of Viet Minh strong points on the "Street without Joy" near Hué. He broke up a troublesome guerrilla battalion operating near Haiphong. From the air he attacked Viet Minh wherever he found them.

By September, as the time for full-scale campaigning was about to open again, the communists had available some 300,000 men, who were organized in part into six regular divisions. They were well supplied with artillery, mortars, recoilless rifles, machine guns, and light automatic weapons.

General Navarre's French Union ground forces at this point totalled about 410,000 troops. At the commanding general's disposal were 230,000 French, of whom 52,000 were Metropolitan French, and 180,000 Vietnamese. The general announced to his troops, "Victory is a woman. She does not give herself except to those who know how to take her."

On November 20th, Navarre seized the small and isolated but strategically located village of Dienbienphu back in the mountains, 175 miles west of Hanoi between the Black River country and Laos. The village straddled a jungle track that led northward to the communist base of Laokay and south to the Laotian capital of Luang Prabang. There the Viet Minh could be made to come to him. Dienbienphu was turned into an entrenched camp.

U.S. AID, AGAIN

In late 1953, there was apparent increased French interest in amphibious operations. General Navarre approved the creation of a Joint Amphibious Command, although actual development of the organization lagged. To augment their capability for landing division-size forces, the French repeated their requests for acceleration in the U.S. effort to deliver naval craft, particularly LSMs (landing ships, medium), LSSLs, and LCUs. But recognizing that they could not be delivered in time to be used in planned amphibious operations, the French requested the loan until December 1954 of several large landing craft to carry out the landings programmed in the Navarre plan.

As a result, the United States expedited delivery of naval craft, including five LSMs, two LSSLs, three LCUs, 40 LCMs, 45 LCVPs, and 70 armored river craft of French design procured in Japan. After receiving assurance that the French could man the additional LSMs without jeopardizing the readiness of other ships, the United States loaned France four additional LSMs.

American naval equipment delivered to the French had already significantly enhanced the French navy's ability to perform its mission in Indochina. The 550 craft programmed for, or delivered to, the French under the Mutual Defense Assistance Programs between 1950 and 1953 represented one-third of all naval craft in Indochina. Through the aid program, the French had been able to repair much of the battle damage they had sustained, to fix broken-down equipment, and to replace most obsolete ships, craft, and airplanes.

Once the initial hardware was provided, the primary U.S. interest became that of ensuring optimum use of these items. As a consequence, the naval aid programs for fiscal years 1952 and 1953 placed considerable emphasis on the provision of logistic support. Exotic no, but needed.

The FY 1952 and 1953 programs included, therefore, major assistance to the French naval shipyard in Saigon and equipment for the repair facility at the Haiphong Naval Amphibious Base. An LST modified as a repair ship was transferred, as were such specialized yard craft as tugs, water and fuel barges, and floating cranes.[3]

Let it not be thought that there were no problems with the generally successful aid program. Aircraft carrier *Bois Belleau* is a case in point. Owing to the time taken to provide a qualified French crew, *Bois Belleau* did not reach France until December 1953, two and a half months later than originally planned. From there things only got worse.

At reactivation, *Bois Belleau*'s boilers were found to be in very poor condition, necessitating drydocking her. The need for additional repairs caused further delay. So did the subsequent French use of the ship to deliver planes to India. The French army would be badly in need of her air support that winter and spring, but the carrier was not to arrive off Indochina until April 30, 1954.[4]

At the end of 1953, the navy section of the Military Assistance Advisory Group, Indochina, assessed the French naval capabilities. Rather than a lack of proficiency on the part of individual personnel or shortage of equipment, the major shortcomings, as seen by the MAAG, were the scarcity of qualified personnel and the long-overdue need for a strong Vietnamese navy. With French laws prohibiting conscripts from serving in Vietnam, only a strong Vietnamese navy could alleviate the chronic personnel shortage in FNEO.[5]

NAVARRE'S OFFENSIVE (OPERATION *ATLANTE*)

On December 12, 1953, General Navarre had notified his subordinate commanders of his decision to launch the promised offensive. His target stretched along the coast from south of Tourane to north of Nha Trang and westward to the mountains along the Laotian and Cambodian borders. In addition to the political apparatus extending down the pyramid of zones, provinces, districts, inter-villages, and villages, the Viet Minh now had an estimated 30,000 troops there.

Prior French operations in this area had been of the hit-and-run variety and had not established continuous control. In *Atlante*, as his overall campaign was called, Navarre planned to move up the coast, establishing bases in three or four successive operations.

Tasks would involve finding and destroying the enemy, detecting and eliminating traps and mines, installing a military police and administrative system, repairing roads and bridges, and carrying out general public reconstruction. By this means he intended to establish firm control over the populated narrow lowland region along the coast from Cape Varella to Fai Fo. In addition to its political value, the area was the main channel for supplies and personnel, either along Route 1 and the railroad, or waterborne off the coast.

Called *Arethuse*, the first phase of this offensive consisted of the seizure of Tuy Hoa by a joint army-navy amphibious assault and subsequent operations from a base area to be established there. The assaulting amphibious force, including LSTs and merchant ships from Tourane, was assembled at Nha Trang under the command of the captain of landing ship dock *La Foudre*. The overall force included a transport group, a landing force, and a naval support group.

The transport group consisted of LSD *La Foudre*, LSTs *Rance* and *Chéliff*, and the Tourane merchant ships. *Foudre* carried the LCMs and LCVPs in her well-deck. Without them, there would be no opposed landing on a hostile beach.

The landing force was made up of two parachute battalions, two navy commando units (*Jaubert* and *Montfort*), an army commando unit, a 75-mm recoilless rifle battalion, a 105-mm artillery battery, an airfield engineer company, artillerymen, and pioneers.

Colonial gunboat *Dumont D'Urville*; two patrol craft, *Commandant Duboc* and *L'Inconstant*; a seaplane tender, *Commandant Robert Giraud*; and an *Aéronavale* (naval air) detachment of Grumman Goose amphibian aircraft formed the naval support group.

On January 19, 1954, part of this force conducted an amphibious demonstration off Quinhon to fix Viet troops stationed in the area, and then headed south during the night to rejoin the rest. The next day—as army forces from Nha Trang advanced along Route 1 and troops from the mountain plateau headed east to open Route 7—the amphibious landing commenced. Weather conditions were favorable except for a low cloud ceiling. As spotters in two Grumman Goose aircraft directed preparatory gunfire from the navy ships, the first wave of landing craft entered the lagoon and landed commandos and engineers on the northern bank of the Da Rang River. In the afternoon another landing was conducted, this time on the south bank.

No serious opposition was encountered, although mine clearance operations ashore slowed the advance. Two hours after the initial landing on the dried-mud flats, Commando *Montfort*, with air support by a Grumman Goose, seized the bridge approaches at Cung Son on Route 7 to the west of Tuy Hoa. By evening the beachhead was well established; Tuy Hoa was under French control. That night the ships furnished continuous star shell illumination, assisting the defense.

Although beach conditions frustrated the landing of field artillery on the 21st, the guns were landed successfully the next day. Commandos continued to guard the bridge and its approaches until the force coming down from the plateau arrived on January 24th. With the amphibious phase of *Arethuse* completed, Tuy Hoa would serve as a logistics base for what was to be a three-month campaign along the coast and into the highlands.[6]

NOTES

1. Edwin B. Hooper, Dan C. Allard, and Oscar P. Fitzgerald, *The United States Navy and the Vietnam Conflict: The Setting of the Stage to 1959* (Washington, D.C.: Naval History Division, 1976), pp. 191–93.
2. Ibid., pp. 193–97.
3. Ibid., pp. 224–26.
4. Pierre Barjot, *Histoire de la Guerre Aéronavale* (Paris: Flammarion, 1961), pp. 402–05.
5. Hooper, Allard, and Fitzgerald, op. cit., p. 226.
6. Ibid., pp. 237–41.

6

DIENBIENPHU AND AFTER

DIENBIENPHU

The situation in general as of mid-February 1954 was that the French held the delta and hill towns and cities but could not clear the jungles and forests, and the Viets held the latter but could not normally storm the towns. The French ruled the day, the guerrillas the night. Both sides were maneuvering for advantage. Nobody could afford to make any serious mistakes.

On the 13th of March, 40,000 Viet Minh—four divisions—who had been building up their strength all winter, at last opened their attack on Dienbienphu and its 15,000 defenders. The limited garrison had not been able to occupy the outlying high hills, and enemy artillery—well dug in, heavily protected by massed light AA guns—dominated the position from the first day. It was the French who tripped.

Supply convoys, more and more frequent now that almost the whole of delta resupply—including that for Dienbienphu—moved by water, soaked up practically all of the khaki navy's available ships and craft. There were few left free for offensive operations of their own. But the river and canal routes between Haiphong and Hanoi had become the supply jugular for the French in the north. This supply had to come first.

THE NAVAL AIR ARM (*AÉRONAVALE*)

The military situation reaching a crisis as it was, the navy did not hesitate to send out almost the last of *Aéronavale*'s metropolitan combat reserve. France's carriers, however, were forced to operate from the Tonkin Gulf, far from the army's highland battles. This fact may have been initially overlooked by the army's high command. Supporting naval air squadrons were thus temporarily landed, flying from the air force's delta air bases.

The French continued to call for more and more American equipment, particularly aircraft. Commander FNEO—Auboyneau again—suggested to Navarre that he request the use of 24 idle pilots from carrier *La Fayette*, then drydocked in France, to fly new F4U-4 Corsair fighter-bombers that might be provided by the U.S. Navy from stocks in the western Pacific.

Navarre duly requested these *La Fayette* pilots, because the *Aéronavale* was conducting the vast majority of the sorties being flown in support of Dienbienphu. The higher instrument qualifications of naval aviators and the better instrument capabilities of their aircraft made them more suited than those of the air force to the task at hand. Support missions in the poor weather that so often enveloped the far-off mountain valley in the spring were in any case a sometime thing.

Within a week of their arrival, *Aéronavale* pilots began flying the Corsairs in support of Dienbienphu. They went into battle just in time to bolster *Arromanches*'s badly depleted squadrons, down to two-thirds of their original strength. On April 30th, carrier *Bois Belleau* finally arrived on station to augment the air effort. In praise of the naval air arm, Navarre later declared that it was the only military service which met and surpassed its obligations at this time of crisis.

Other aid also continued to flow to Indochina. In May, the French obtained a second squadron of ten Privateer long-range maritime patrol planes.

FNEO had no helicopters. Many were the short-range humanitarian logistic and medical evacuation missions flown by *Aéronavale*'s U.S.-furnished small Sea Otters, military and civilian.[1] The navy made do here, too.

THE FALL

In the *métropole*, the French will to fight for their Indochinese patrimony had gradually over the years been sapped by France's continuing heavy losses and the eventual drafting of conscripts to serve out there. For some, there were moral questions, too, about what appeared to be the imposition of an alien government on a people wanting to be free. The communist hard core and the brutal terrorism of the Viet Minh were easily overlooked when they had to be. A major disaster at Dienbienphu would prove to be the last straw.

The fall of Dienbienphu and the collapse of French power in the north came nonetheless with numbing suddenness.

An international conference had been called to convene in Geneva in May to wind up both the Korean and the Indochinese wars. It was Indochina that headed the agenda.

Ordered to do nothing under any circumstances that would disturb the preliminary armistice negotiations then ongoing at Geneva, General Navarre was allowed to make no serious effort to relieve Dienbienphu. He might have been able to do so. He did have some 20 battalions available, including four airborne battalions in the northern delta. A small relief column was actually sent from Luang Prabang, but was too small to do more than harass the communist besiegers.

As early as February, the possibility of U.S. combat air strikes in support of Dienbienphu was under discussion by the allies.

Two—later three—U.S. attack carriers took up positions in the Tonkin Gulf. Preparatory reconnaissance missions were flown. But the Americans would not act except together with the British, and this time they opted out. The French were left to go it alone.

Dienbienphu fell May 7th, after 55 days of siege. For the gallant defenders, the torture had ended. As the Viets overwhelmed the position, de Castries radioed Hanoi, *"Au revoir, mon général. Vive la France!"* It was a *beau geste*, but that was all. The day that Dienbienphu fell, the Geneva conference formally opened.

CONSEQUENCES

By mid-May, Giap's troops, now a triumphant army, smelled blood. They streamed east down Route Coloniale No. 1, 80 miles from Hanoi, headed for the delta. They knew, and the French were painfully aware, that Dienbienphu had used up a very large percentage of the French reserves. They came for the kill.

On the 8th of June, General Paul Ely, from Paris, replaced Navarre, becoming the eighth c in c in Indochina since 1945. He was also appointed commissioner-general, representing the French government.

In the delta, the war continued. By mid-June, Giap had concentrated eight regular Viet Minh divisions against the 300-mile delta perimeter. Two infantry and one heavy weapons division were deployed on the north and two on the south. The equivalent of three divisions was infiltrated into the delta itself. Total communist strength was 110,000 regulars and up to 200,000 irregulars, all with the highest morale.

Major General René Cogny, commanding the northern delta front, had at his disposal between 70,000 and 100,000 troops. Approximately a quarter were French and the rest were Vietnamese.

The latter part of June and the first part of July, French forces closed up to protect Hanoi, evacuating all of the southern one-third of the delta. The idea now was to hold on to something as a political bargaining chip, and just perhaps to serve as a base for further action if the Geneva talks failed, minimizing losses.

OPERATION *AUVERGNE*

The final French evacuation of the southern zone and the withdrawal behind the Red River was dubbed Operation *Auvergne*. It involved the clearing of Nam Dinh and the several posts that bordered the Red River between Nam Dinh Giang and the Cua Balat. At the same time, the Phat Diem sector was to be evacuated via the Day.

To be pulled out of the southern zone were not only troops and their equipment, but also the maximum number of loyal civilians and their goods and chattels without producing defections among the Vietnamese units. Involved were three LSSLs, several LCTs, and the craft of three *dinassauts*.

In order to deceive the enemy, the French organized a parallel cover operation. This was meant to convince the Viets that the movements under way were only a regrouping of forces and a new division of territorial responsibilities between the French and the locals. No unnecessary risks were to be taken.

The withdrawal followed three different axes. The forces from the Phat Diem sector were loaded on light craft under enemy fire and then evacuated by the Day to the sea.

The evacuations from Thai Binh and Bui Chu were also effected by the river and sea, on the axis Nam Dinh-Van Mon-mouth of the Red River, without opposition.

As the southern zone was evacuated and remaining forces consolidated, the tired and worn out *dinassauts* again came to the fore. These were difficult and dangerous operations. Both the rescuers and the rescued were vulnerable to Viet action. The big LSSLs could not always come upstream far enough to provide support. Commandos had to land and hold the riverbanks, at least partially, for the few hours necessary for the approach and withdrawal of the landing craft. They had to lay on ready artillery support or a combat air patrol.

The evacuees had then to be embarked in haste, along with as much materiel as possible. So had their dependents and other civilians desiring to leave. So had their cattle and fowl; the rest had to be destroyed. Inevitably, there were ambushes and losses.

The principal effort—and also the most delicate—concerned the withdrawal of the troops and civilians from Ninh Binh and Nam Dinh in the direction of Phu Ly. By the 1st of July, all these movements were completed and the evacuated troops established around Phu Ly.

One convoy was ambushed during withdrawal, caught under heavy weapons fire. Almost all the craft were damaged and some had to be left behind. One LCM (Bremont, commanding), having already safely run the gauntlet, turned around, collected the survivors and their weapons from the wrecked craft, and came back out, still under Viet fire. She had been closely supported by a lone LCT (de Villier, commanding) mounting a 120-mm mortar, but that was all. Bremont succeeded in rejoining the convoy, where he caught a dressing down for his action![2]

The withdrawal left the densely populated and rich rice-producing area south of the Red River, 1,600 square miles and 2,500,000 people, to the control of the Viets. Nam Dinh, Phu Ly, and Phat Diem had been surrendered. The French reorganized behind an intricate series of rivers and canals on a line 100 miles shorter and more easily defended.

The French essentially now held only a strip along both sides of the Hanoi–Haiphong corridor. They also held a narrow coastal strip around the Campha mines, in the north of Along Bay.

At the same time, in view of the Geneva negotiations, General Ely was ordered by Paris to establish communication with the enemy. French staff officers met the communists in the small village of Trunggia, 25 miles northwest of Hanoi, beginning July 4th. There they worked out technical questions relating to a ceasefire.

The delta being almost completely abandoned, there was no longer a question of large-scale riverine operations. Craft belonging to the *dinassauts*, as well as the LSSLs and the LCTs, were regrouped at Haiphong. The LCTs were kept busy moving materiel and people about, but the LSSLs had only a minuscule transport capacity and escaped this logistic activity. The LSSLs were used on occasional liaison missions to the ships anchored in Along Bay and to patrol navigation channels.

CEASEFIRE

On the 21st of July, 1954, after seven years and seven months of bloody war, the formal conflict between the French Union forces and the Viet Minh ended with the signing of three truce agreements.

Generally the terms provided that the line of demarcation between communist and Free Vietnam should be along the Ben Hai River, roughly at the 17th Parallel. French Union forces, being required to evacuate northern Vietnam, were given 80 days to leave Hanoi and 300 days to leave Haiphong. All organized Viet Minh in the south were required to assemble in five areas within 200 days for evacuation to the north.

The territorial integrity of Cambodia and of Laos, except for two areas in the northeast corner, was to be respected by the Viets. Cambodia and Laos were to retain only those forces needed for self-defense. Limited French military units were also allowed to remain.

Ho Chi Minh, supported by China's Mao Tse-tung, had won control over 77,000 square miles of land and more than half of the people of Vietnam. The fragment of a government remaining in the south only nominally administered the remaining 50,000 square miles of territory.

The news of the ceasefire was, of course, no surprise to the *dinassauts*, but the blow was nonetheless hard to bear. So many losses to arrive here . . . In the course of the last twelve months of the war, of 40 officers consigned to the amphibious forces in Tonkin, six were killed and 12 wounded, three seriously. The survivors understood the relief of their families, but they were unable to avoid the idea that they were abandoning all those people to a regime the character of which was evidenced by a mounting stream of refugees.[3]

In any case, the LCTs ran no risk of being idle. In the course of the next months, Haiphong was to see passing through so many people and so much materiel that the port itself could not handle it. The greater part of them had to be rerouted to Along Bay. It was the LCTs that regularly operated the shuttle between the port proper and the ships at their anchorages in the bay.

A required final exchange of prisoners began in mid-August at Viet Tri. It was the navy's LCTs that received the French POWs, giving up their loads of Viets in exchange. It was the navy that carried the prisoners to safety.

Sixty-three thousand prisoners of war were returned to the Viet Minh. Of the 36,979 French carried as missing in action since 1945, 10,754 were returned by the Viets. This is a mere 28 percent of the total.

Of the returned French, half (6,132) had immediately to be hospitalized in a physical state which recalled that of the survivors of Buchenwald. In addition to the extreme physical punishment they received, the French had undergone courses of "re-education"—really brainwashing—which involved a slow degradation of the individual's spirit.[4]

CLOSING OUT

Landing craft transport *La Foudre* finally came north for the last time. It was there to pick up the *dinassauts*' boats. There remained in Haiphong only those ships capable of sailing south on their own—LSSLs, LSILs, LCIs, and LCTs.

The day of departure, the LSSLs—as at Nam Dinh—descended the Cua Cam last. At the anchorage, they picked up the transports that had loaded the army's rearguard. The next morning, in small groups, they all left for the south. Garnier's tricolor no longer flew over Hanoi.

The Tonkin ships reassembled at the anchorage off Cape St. Jacques. In order to preserve what face they could, the ships entered Saigon in impeccable formation, manning yards and rails. It was a fitting end to the whole dirty war.[5]

As of December 1954, under then-existing agreements, France had retained ultimate military responsibility for the security of Free Indochina. General Ely still headed the French Union command. However, the unpopular French Expeditionary Corps, then 125,000 strong, was to be further reduced to 70,000 in gradual withdrawals. In two years they would all be gone.

Free Vietnam's forces were still not in a position to maintain internal security. Viet Minh agents who were ordered to stay behind continued to operate in hinterland areas technically free. The shaky Vietnamese army, then 217,000, was to be cut to a constabulary of 90,000 picked officers and men. As reorganized and retrained, it would not have been capable of resisting an invasion from the north but might have been able to cope with small-scale terrorism.

The French (and the United States) in Indochina had suffered a major defeat. At Dienbienphu, the deciding battle, Navarre confidently gambled the greater part of his reserves in a decisive battle, and lost. World politics and internal French loss of interest did the rest at Geneva.

Victory had given herself, not to the deserving, but to those who knew how to take her.

NOTES

1. Jean-Pierre Gomane, *Les Marins et L'Outre-Mer* (Paris: Denoël, 1988), pp. 147–49.
2. Bernard Estival, *L'Enseigne dans le Delta* (Versailles: Editions les 7 Vents, 1989), pp. 167–72.
3. Ibid., pp. 175–76.
4. Ibid., p. 211.
5. Ibid., pp. 221–22.

CONCLUSION

The success of French colonial rule in Indochina had always flowed from their adoption of a maritime strategy. This was supported right from the beginning by a naval force capable of conducting operations promptly and in sufficient force, moving troops swiftly to trouble spots, dominating the sea lanes adjacent and leading to Indochina, and controlling inland waters. As long as this sea power remained strong in the Far East, French interests in Indochina prospered.

Then between 1940 and 1945, the metropolitan source of the sea power required to support such a strategy dried up. In Indochina the Japanese first took over militarily, then, on March 9, 1945, totally destroyed the colonial administrative structure. French rule died.

With the defeat of the Japanese in the summer of 1945, the British in the south and the Nationalist Chinese in the north temporarily took over the occupation of Indochina. The British in their zone brought back the French and promptly withdrew.

In the north, however, only after prolonged negotiation did the Chinese finally evacuate and permit the French Expeditionary Corps to replace them.

During 1946 the returning French, reassuming the government, worked frantically to recover the foundations of power. They soon found that cooperation with the Viet Minh was impossible. The communists turned on the French in Hanoi and other places in the north in December 1946. Paris decided that the only solution would have to be one of a military nature.

The fundamental French strategy had always been clear. Under this strategy, first priority continued to be assigned to the two main deltas (Mekong and Red) and to the intervening coastal regions. These were the most densely populated areas, the locations of cities, the most fertile lands, the centers of what industry there was, trade, and communications. These regions provided the country with most of its food. These were also the areas where naval power—in all its forms—could be brought to bear. The French occasionally raided more remote parts of the country, but these raids were considered of only secondary importance. When in 1953 the French violated this strategy by occupying Dienbienphu, an isolated outpost in the mountains far inland, the results were a disaster.

After the Chinese communists reached the Tonkin border, the French were confronted with an enemy that could draw endlessly upon the communists' vast military resources. At this point, Paris offered Vietnam, Laos, and Cambodia political autonomy within a French Union, granting them all that had been demanded in 1946, but then it was too late. The Viet Minh were no longer dependent upon the attractions of nationalism to sustain their movement. The rebellion gradually assumed all of the characteristics of a formal war.

Enter de Lattre. He exercised authority over both the civilian and military administration and placed into effect his plan for a reasoned approach to the problem in Indochina. De Lattre crushed the rebels' delta offensive within six months, and Ho returned to guerrilla warfare. For a year, de Lattre skillfully stemmed the

CONCLUSION

rising tide of communist power, and it began to appear that an acceptable solution might yet be possible. When he died, the communists regained the initiative, and within another year the French position was again deteriorating. In Indochina, for the French to go on the defensive was for them to await defeat.

Victory was nowhere in sight. The consequences of defeat were becoming apparent. "Who loses Hanoi loses Algiers" was a phrase heard more and more frequently in the navy's warrooms and reflected in its spirit. This foreboding drove it to always one more great effort, always at greater cost.

Navarre assumed command in Indochina early in 1953. He instituted his own vigorous plan for a solution, but by this time Ho's forces were too strong. The loss of Dienbienphu and its 15,000-man garrison brought about a crisis which the French, since 1945 reluctant to face the issue, could not surmount.

The northern half of Vietnam was turned over to the communists in a truce settlement signed at Geneva in 1954, and the French left altogether soon after.

There are several purely military lessons to be learned or relearned from the unhappy experience of the French. The first and most important is that in putting down a rebellion such as the one in Indochina, where the paramount military problem could not reasonably be separated from the political one, the principle of unit of command cannot be ignored. When de Lattre was given control over both the military and the civil authority, including the police, French affairs prospered.

There were other lessons. The spectacular results obtained by de Lattre in the short period he held command, especially when contrasted with what followed, emphasize that the historically important value of inspired leadership has not diminished in a modern force. Even the khaki navy felt this.

THE INFLUENCE OF SEA POWER

Vietnam's geography made the area particularly susceptible to the influence of sea power. Even when the many indentations and promontories are not included, the coast measures some 1,500 miles from the Chinese border in the north to Cambodia in the south. As narrow as 30 miles at one point, the S-shaped strip of land that now comprises Vietnam has an average width of only 80 miles.

For nine years the *Marine Nationale* supported an expeditionary corps of from 120,000 to 150,000 men fighting 7,000 miles from home. For these years, out of an overall naval personnel of 58,000 men, the navy kept 10,000 to 12,000 men in Indochina, despite tensions in Europe and other places.

The French navy was not directly challenged in Indochina either at sea or in the air. It was thus from the first enabled to close the coast, instituting a close blockade of enemy-held areas, and providing air and shore bombardment support from the sea. It was able to pursue the enemy up the rivers and streams and into the swamps and marshes.

Thus, as the French themselves pointed out, owing to the peculiar geography of the country the French navy found itself fighting as far into the interior as its means would take it. There were, therefore, six principal missions of the French navy in the war in Indochina:

1. to control the coast in order to provide freedom of access and maneuver;
2. to interdict coastal waters to the enemy;
3. to clear mines from ports and waterways;
4. to use naval aviation for patrol, precision bombing, and direct support of naval forces;
5. to clear and hold the network of interior waterways that serve as the principal means of access to the life of the country;
6. to support the other forces, operationally and logistically.

Every one was pursued to the hilt.

RIVERINE WARFARE

Nothing naval runs through the Indochina story like the *dinassauts*. In 1945, FNEO boasted a 35,000-ton fast battleship; by

CONCLUSION

1950, there were none. In the early years, the *Aéronavale* was hardly there; by 1954, there were two light aircraft carriers playing a major operational role. But the river flotillas were always there. They were the natural answer to a need that could not otherwise be met.

The tempo of French riverine operations increased steadily from 1946 until the end. *Dinassauts* played an absolutely key role in the battles for the Red River delta in 1951 and 1952. Major battles were fought at Ninh Binh (May–June 1951) and at Hoa Binh (November 1951–February 1952). By the end, the *dinassauts* were fully committed and taking heavy casualties. No one could imagine doing without them.

Even the earlier *dinassaut* missions demonstrated some of the general lessons that the French derived from their experiences in riverine combat. As at Gian Khau on the night of February 2, 1948, naval mobility often gave the French the element of operational surprise. That was the first thing.

The French plans for the expected ambush indicated also their respect for the enemy's use of controlled mines, that often initiated an ambush, or that, in many instances, were employed in conjunction with barricades thrown across waterways to obstruct river movement. Yet actual attacks revealed the tendency of the Viet Minh to vitiate the effectiveness of their firepower by failing to concentrate it. French counterattacks demonstrated the importance of responding as quickly as possible with a concentrated and heavy volume of fire.

The French at first had no choice but to make use in riverine operations of whatever ships and craft were available. Later on, they produced a purpose-designed 36-foot patrol boat known as the STCAN/FOM. Most of their craft, however, remained those of British and American design produced during World War II, with added armor and guns. These proved generally adequate, even though more speed and firepower would always have been welcome, especially when moving against current and tide.

Mines, automatic weapons, and bazookas were the Viet Minh arms of choice. But there is no doubt that in respect of danger to *ships* the mine posed the biggest threat. *Personnel* suffered largely from bazooka fire and mortars. The use of flamethrowers against close-in ambush was advocated by the French naval command but not really tried on any scale before the war ended.

The war in Indochina, sad as it was and humiliating in its ultimate consequences, was conducted by the *Marine Nationale* as a sort of personal affair, reflecting Indochina's geography and the weight of long historical association. It there dedicated a weight of effort totally disproportionate to its means. This is not less true of the *Aéronavale* than of the surface navy.

Although all sorts of navies have frequently been asked to assure permanently the use of threatened waterways whose banks were in friendly hands, and although these have been charged temporarily to assure the security of waterways whose shores were in enemy hands, never before had any navy been asked permanently to assure the security or use of rivers and canals whose banks were hostile. This was the achievement of the "khaki navy."

AMPHIBIOUS RAIDS

The French were convinced that conducting small-scale amphibious raids against Viet supply points along the coast was one effective means of interdicting the enemy's logistics. These operations resulted in a number of successes in destroying small enemy craft beached on the coast or the personnel facilities and supply depots that supported these units.

Nevertheless, one of the frustrating aspects of such operations was the continuing ability of the enemy to escape before contact was made. No one disappeared as quickly or as well as a Viet. For this reason French tacticians emphasized the need for the utmost speed of execution directly against predetermined locations of enemy forces. These authorities noted that encirclement tactics, in the face of the enemy's skillful ability to avoid combat when it was in his interest to do so, were not always successful either.

The Nam Dinh convoys brings up another point. The French navy complained that the army officers who controlled naval operations in Indochina tended to use river forces all too seldom for aggressive strikes at the enemy. Instead, they claimed, the army favored patrols to secure lines of communication and logistic support.

In addition to noting the relative lack of outright assault missions, critiques of the war concluded that the full effectiveness of river assault divisions was hampered by the usual absence of integral landing forces of sufficient strength.

As a result, one of the major naval recommendations emerging from the war called for the establishment of an amphibious corps under a single commander, composed of necessary riverine craft, sizable ground forces, and artillery. It was further suggested that this force, foreshadowing the Mobile Riverine Force later established by the United States in its Vietnam War, should be assigned the responsibility for maintaining security within a specified territorial zone.

Realistic appraisals by the French of the shortcomings of their river forces included several other recommendations. They suggested above all specially constructed river craft with greater speed and armament than the converted Allied landing craft that typically were used.

The French further acknowledged the enemy's abilities. He could plan devastating ambushes of French river forces, exploiting support and intelligence gained from the local people. He was on the other hand ingenious in using the watercraft and the waterways to break out of the most carefully planned French traps. These skills made him a difficult enemy indeed.

THE BOTTOM LINE

The creation of the *dinassauts* may well have been one of the few worthwhile contributions to military knowledge of the Indochina war. One senior French army commander, who had a direct appreciation of these forces, summarized the importance of their role. He saw it as the creation, for the first time, of a flexible, strategic instrument, thanks to the diversity of its materiel, capable of riverine action without being limited by the needs of territorial security.

It would seem that essentially the French lost Indochina because of factors off their military radar. History was against them. Times had changed in the Far East, and the French had not. They could never really understand why a force of 200 men could not handle any problems that arose in 1954 as well as it had those that arose in 1874.

It would appear that there were three reasons why this could not be done. First, there was Indochinese nationalism, a relatively recent phenomenon, which the French simply did not comprehend. Second, guerrilla warfare had been scientifically developed to the point that unimaginatively applied countermeasures only worked to the advantage of the guerrillas. Third, the French greatly underestimated the driving strength of communist ideology and policy. This could not be stopped by clay forts or concrete bunkers—or *dinassauts*—a fact which the best leaders soon realized.

The French navy in Indochina was a wholly professional one, organized and equipped along Western lines. It fought well; there can be no question of that. It was fighting, unfortunately, something that guns alone could not settle. The tragedy is that so many good men of all ranks tried so hard and gave so much, accomplished so little, and were in the end abandoned to defeat.

In this war for Indochina, unlike the situation a hundred years earlier, however, naval power could not be decisive. This war was fundamentally a land war and, above all, a guerrilla war. But it *was* also a war in the mud, the flooded deltas, and the rivers.

The French navy met all requirements levied upon it, skillfully adapting its ships, craft, and techniques to action across rice paddies and through mangrove swamps. That the war was not won is no reflection on the navy. Its annals will forever list the

CONCLUSION

valiant efforts of the *dinassauts*, the river flotillas, and the little ships with the romantic names.

On the small ships, "taps" is a simple ceremony. So Quartermaster, strike a slow eight on the bell! Strike it for "les anciens," sick, in rags and tatters, badly armed, who fought with so much honor in Saigon in 1945. Strike it for Vilar, for Jaubert, for Kermadec. And for all the others of the khaki navy "mort pour la France" in the stinking jungles and tangled swamps, doing their duty. Slowly, Quartermaster. Slowly. The defeat was not theirs.

EPILOGUE

THE BEGINNINGS OF A VIETNAMESE NAVY

It was through the (South) Vietnamese navy that the concept of *dinassaut* was passed on. The Vietnamese navy first surfaced in the Franco-Vietnamese military agreement of December 30, 1949. This agreement called for the French to provide a cadre for a navy and to furnish basic training and advanced instruction for it. Only a river navy was proposed in Admiral Ortoli's April 1950 preliminary plan.

Except for these plans, little progress was made. Concerned over the delays, the Naval Ministry in Paris insisted on action.

The Indochinese-command French had serious reservations about all this. De Lattre wanted to create a single Vietnamese armed service, and did not initially agree with the concept of a separate navy. Ortoli had his own reservations. He was afraid that the manning of a Vietnamese navy would interfere with recruitment of Vietnamese for the French navy in Indochina.

In November 1951, construction of the Recruit Training Center alongside Nha Trang's deep-water bay began. A training course for deck and engineering officers was at the same time established on board a French ship.

On March 6, 1952, Chief of State Bao Dai signed an ordnance providing for the official establishment of a Vietnamese navy. The French took a tangible step toward such a navy when they added a naval department to their military mission.

Although over two years had gone by since the original decision to establish a new navy, little progress had been made with the foremost problem—the personnel to man the force. To meet the requirements of FNEO itself—then limited by a 10,000-man ceiling on French nationals because of a ban on the use of draftees overseas and by demands elsewhere—some 400 Vietnamese had been recruited directly into the French navy. Although these locally recruited men received some training, they were assigned only to auxiliary units, small landing craft attached to army units, and nonrated duties with the French river forces. They would be little help.

The training problems were formidable. Although may Vietnamese indeed lived along the coast and the inland waterways and earned their living from fishing or operating small craft, those with a technical education were few and illiteracy was common. Faced with heavy commitments to their own operations, the French were understandably reluctant to divert any of their limited resources to creating the new navy.

Two programs were initiated to acquire the necessary officers. A starting cadre would be obtained through accelerated training of selected university graduates. Longer term policy was to run cadets through established French naval schools.

The Nha Trang Training Center was approaching completion. The initial class (150 apprentice seamen and 25 petty officer candidates, including some who had served in the French Union forces) were admitted in June 1952. The center opened officially in July.

Progress toward realization of a Vietnamese navy nonetheless continued at a slow pace. A Franco-Vietnamese decision in February 1953 recommended a supplemental naval program to include three additional river flotillas (each composed of LCTs, LCMs, LCVPs, sampans, and river patrol boats), one LST, and four LSSLs. The program remained under discussion for the rest of 1953.

At this point, Admiral Auboyneau, back as commander FNEO, proposed development of a complete riverine amphibious capability for the new navy by organizing naval infantry units, similar to the *Fusiliers Marins*. A Vietnamese marine corps was finally established, in October 1954.

A NAVY OF THEIR OWN

In April 1953, at long last, the first Vietnamese naval unit was activated. The unit—a *dinassaut*—consisted of only five landing craft, armed and equipped with 50-caliber and 20-mm guns. It was one of two organized that year for operations in the Mekong delta. Although partially manned by French cadres and under French command, the craft flew the Vietnamese flag. This unit was based at Can Tho, at the junction of the Bassac and Can Tho rivers. The second Vietnamese *dinassaut* was formed in the summer and based at Vinh Long.

Encouraging as these first steps were, the Vietnamese had much to do before they could develop an effective navy. The navy was placed under the predominantly army-manned Armed Forces Joint General Staff. This staff controlled the single budget covering all military services. Naval personnel were but a tiny portion of the total armed forces, representing only about one-half of one percent. Furthermore, the French and the Vietnamese pushed differing naval programs. Naval representation was thus not only weak but divided.

In early 1954, the French resumed the transfer of ships. They turned over to the Vietnamese three motor minesweepers, in ceremonies at Saigon in February. A third *dinassaut* was established in March and a fourth in August.

Despite their avowed intention to increase the combat role of the Vietnamese navy, particularly under the ill-starred Navarre Plan, the French otherwise had made little real progress. When the war ended, the Vietnamese navy operated only one LSIL, one LCU, and some 30 smaller amphibious craft. Further, the navy was commanded by a French officer, and most of the other key posts were held by Frenchmen.

FNEO was disestablished on April 26, 1956. As the proud French slowly departed Indochina for good, the United States required them to leave behind all of their Vietnam war aid for Vietnamese use.

During the next years, the new navy burgeoned at long last. The navy soon gained operational control over its riverine units and replaced French personnel with its own officers and men. The small river force continued to play a crucial role in establishing the writ of the new republic and in putting down various dissident military forces. It was continually in action.

The avowed aim now was to develop a small, highly efficient naval organization, one capable of limited amphibious operations, river and coastal patrol, minesweeping, direct fire support, and logistic support. It was for the day a realistic goal. It assumed time enough to accomplish it.

Soon there were three operational divisions to the new navy: a river force, a sea force, and a marine force.

By 1957, the navy had increased to 4,800 men. River force craft had increased by 50 percent. The river force counted six *dinassauts*, with units based at My Tho, Cat Lo, Vinh Long, Cat Lai, Can Tho, and Long Xuyen. The marines mustered six river companies (one for each *dinassaut*) and one battalion landing team.

By 1959, the period of low-level conflict with the north—a war that had never stopped—began to change its character. Guerrilla actions in the south again approached a state of insurgency. Full-scale war was back.

By the 1960s, thanks to a development program put into effect during the last years of the French, the Mekong delta had become the rice bowl of the south, feeding Saigon and exporting the considerable surplus. By 1964, large amounts were starting to be diverted to feed the communist guerrillas (now called the Viet Cong). This had to be stopped.

By 1966, however, as the United States began its direct intervention, the navy's time had run out. Vietnamese *dinassauts* were being used in their primary role only ten percent of the time. The Vietnamese army apparently preferred using helicopters to landing craft for the assault. *Dinassauts* were therefore employed mainly in support of local small unit operations, or simply as escorts for commercial craft.

THE DAY OF THE YANKEE

The U.S. Navy was to follow in the wake of the French and then extend their techniques and equipment, for themselves and for the Vietnamese. The Americans had taken up the training, equipping, and advising of the south's military in 1956, two years after the evacuation of the north. They were to continue this role until 1975. This included the river assault groups (RAGs), as Americans called them.

The United States had to have heard of the *dinassauts*. The French wrote extensively about them. Diplomatic observers reported on them.

By 1961, there were in the south some 8,000 American support troops, many of them navy advisors. While not always ecstatic over the quality of hastily organized Vietnamese units, those advisors with the RAGs told a tale of personal Vietnamese dedication and courage, many of the crews having had long experience in riverine combat. Few listened.

At intervention in 1965, the U.S. Navy was ill-prepared for riverine and coastal warfare. Despite the advisors' years of experience with the RAGs—even when it directly joined the battle—the navy still underestimated the importance of Vietnam's river war. It did not recognize that in the south—as in the north— the waterways were lines of communication to be exploited rather than simply obstacles to be crossed. It learned quickly. Some did, at least.

The navy eventually organized a much larger inshore effort than even the French ever had. This effort was three-pronged: a coastal interdiction force, a river patrol force, and a joint army/navy mobile riverine force to take the fight to the enemy and destroy him. For this MRF, the navy manned the ships and craft, while two brigades of the army's 9th Infantry Division provided the assault troops.

The U.S. deployment onto the rivers was initially really a hurried affair involving much improvisation of equipment, personnel, organization, and tactics. Nonetheless, the MRF—like the *dinassauts* before them—were one of the strategic successes of the American Vietnam War. A good idea is hard to kill.

Still, once U.S. riverine operations were begun, it took three years—from 1965 to 1968—for the navy to penetrate from coastal waters into the mouths of the big rivers, probing the narrower streams, and finally pushing far upstream, past islands and villages, jungle and swamp, asserting waterway control as it went.

In typically American style, in the end they had of course developed a whole new family of river assault ships and craft, only distant cousins to those used by the French. Some of the gunboats, for instance, were armed with flamethrowers and water cannon for use against Viet bunkers. Even patrol boats were equipped with navigational radar. Some had water jet propulsion units. Yes. But the ghosts of those who had served in the *dinassauts*—Jaubert, even—would easily have recognized the tactics.

Saigon fell in 1975, two years after the last U.S. river units had gone.

Nonetheless, thus was the concept of the *dinassaut* passed on, first to the South Vietnamese, then to the watching Americans. Its durability in the face of every kind of political and administrative obstacle speaks for its continuing worth. The *dinassauts* all began with the events outlined on these pages.

APPENDIX A: CONCEPTUAL PROBLEMS OF BLUE WATER NAVIES

The whole problem of inshore operations has bedeviled navies with "blue water" aspirations for years. The French were no exception, struggling with this question all through the Indochina war. Change "French" to "American" and the story could be written about the United States. We can perhaps see things more objectively when we look at another navy.

By 1952 FNEO had shaken itself down and was showing all of the psycho-political problems of a navy tied to the land. There was no longer a *"Marine en Indochine"* because the French navy clung ferociously to a global role. Unfortunately, that pretension to responsibility for large spaces led it often to consider with a certain disdain theaters of operation which appeared too narrow. The navy committed its ships and men to operations ashore only with reluctance.

The navy in Indochina thus ached to be of the whole Far East, not just Indochina, and not without reason. It was indispensable then to show again a French presence in the Pacific after an absence of many years. It was nonetheless difficult to explain to the army, carrying the weight of the war, that a third of the navy spent its time showing off the red pompom in Yokosuka, in Manila, or at Singapore.

This attitude probably sprang in part from a natural reluctance by the navy to allow itself to play inevitable second fiddle to the army ashore. The army had historically always been the larger, was always in modern times in charge of whatever joint operations the military took on, and was therefore in the eyes of the public and the government the most important service. This was especially true at budget time.

It was also possible that there was in this attitude, in part, a reaction to the seductive ideas of the *Jeune École* of the turn of the century. The *Jeune École*'s ideas were designed for a navy destined always to be second best—as against Britain's Royal Navy. It espoused a defensive navy built around raiding cruisers, swarms of coastal torpedo boats, and shore-based coast defenses (mines, guns). The advent of the guided missile boat has given these ideas new life.

In Algeria (1954–62), the navy again put large forces at the disposal of the army in what was essentially a land campaign. There the navy established and was given charge of a maritime frontier zone. Included were naval commandos and *Fusilier Marin* units, although in such terrain no *dinassauts* were called for. The navy itself sited and manned frontier radars to locate and track infiltrators crossing from Morocco and Tunisia. It carried out there the same coastal surveillance maintained shortly before off Tonkin and in the Gulf of Siam. The navy intercepted at least three ships in its net, ships flying neutral flags but stuffed with arms for the rebels. It must have discouraged an unknowable number more. These various activities soaked up some 5,000 always scarce naval personnel.

The specter of a French navy reduced to a mere coastal force never ceases to haunt the nightmares of French admirals. Nelson's far-flung ships upon which Napoleon's Grand Army never set eyes had taught most of them a lesson, too well, perhaps. The problem was not specific to Indochina and was to be found later in Algeria.

APPENDIX B: GEOGRAPHY OF INDOCHINA

Geographically, tropical Indochina properly consists of the whole of the vast peninsula, projecting from the Asiatic land mass between the Indian Ocean and the China Sea, pointing toward the East Indies. The eastern part of the peninsula is called particularly Indochina—in 1945, French Indochina.

Until 1946 French Indochina was made up of five states: the colony of Cochin-China and the protectorates of Annam, Cambodia, Tonkin, and Laos. (Now, 1990, it officially, *de jure*, consists of the three independent states of Vietnam, Cambodia, and Laos.)

From early times history reveals that maritime influence and the application of naval power played decisive roles in shaping the destiny of states in the Indochinese peninsula. This section seeks to provide insight as to how control over the region hinged on riverine and coastal warfare and on the role of naval operations on inland waters.

Furthermore, the course of history has frequently demonstrated Vietnam's strategic importance. Lying along the South China Sea, on a massive peninsula jutting down between Malaya and China, Vietnam occupies a key position alongside one of the most dense shipping lanes of the world. Historically, the relatively narrow span of navigable water between the southeastern coast of Vietnam and the "dangerous ground" further to the east has been the main trade link between Europe, Africa, the Middle East, South Asia, Singapore, Indonesia, Malaya, Thailand, and Cambodia on the one hand, and China, Japan, the Philippines, and additional East Asian countries on the other. Ships in this lane also proceed between Southeast Asia and North America.

Topographically, Indochina is made up basically of two large river deltas and a jagged mountain backbone running the entire length of the country. The mountains, the Annamese Cordillera, or *Chaine Annamite*, are a tumbled 7,000-foot range, with individual peaks reaching as high as 10,000 feet. They possess a rather steep slope on the east but a more gradual one on the west, forming several large plateaus.

The mountainous northern frontier of Indochina, the border between Tonkin and China, has always been of considerable military importance, but it has never been properly surveyed. The frontier is actually marked by a string of old French forts and outposts located on the main north-south routes, connected by a road called then Route Coloniale No. 4, which winds between steep hills and dense forests.

If one looks at a chart of Indochina, the importance of the river war in the fighting becomes immediately apparent. There are two vast deltas; one the delta of Tonkin, which comprises the river systems of the *Rivière Rouge*, the *Noire*, and the *Claire* (picturesque and literal names, the Red, the Black, and the Clear); while in the south, in Cambodia and Cochin-China, there is the delta of the mighty Mekong.

Some French naval officers have gone so far as to estimate that 90 percent of the communications system of Indochina is by water, whether by the China Sea, the rivers and their confluences, or by canal. It is certain that under conditions of the French war where land communications, both by rail and road, were severed by the Viet Minh, the river systems assumed an ever more vital aspect.

The mighty Mekong rises 2,500 miles upstream in the Himalayan Mountains of central Tibet. With a drainage basin larger than the state of Texas, the Mekong proceeds through Yunnan Province of China, forms the border between Laos and Burma and most of Thailand, traverses Cambodia, and at Phnom Penh divides into two arms extending to the South China Sea—the Mekong and the Bassac. Crisscrossed by innumerable waterways, almost the entire region south of Saigon and much of Cambodia consist of a vast delta, the "rice bowl of Asia,"

APPENDIX B

formed by the accumulation of silt brought down by the Mekong and its tributaries.

In the south, the winters are the good time. Extensive regions of the delta are inundated during the summer months, a result of heavy tropical rains caused by the moisture brought from the Indian Ocean by the southwest monsoonal winds.

In the north, where the northeast monsoon brings the fall-to-spring rainy season, the predominant waterway is the Red River, which rises in Yunnan Province and is navigable all the way from the sea to the Chinese border. The rice-rich delta formed by this river and its tributaries is the most densely populated region of Vietnam and the site of its capital, Hanoi.

Delta terrain is complex: a network of twisted creeks, dense jungle, and hot, humid swamps, dikes, soggy rice paddy fields, and scattered island-like villages edged with mangrove, nipa palm, bamboo, and banana trees. The rice paddies are crossed by a maze of twisting streams, connected here and there by a canal. During the monsoon rains, the deltas flood, and the *only* practicable means of transport is by water.

APPENDIX C: WEATHER

Weather in Indochina exerted a major influence on military actions, particularly air operations in the north. Late September is the beginning of the autumnal transition from the southwest to the northeast monsoon. Soon thereafter, cooling of the northern part of the vast continent of Asia develops a wide, high-pressure area, that increases in intensity. In the Northern Hemisphere, the air spirals clockwise out of the high-pressure area. Although cold and dry at the source region over China, the northeast monsoon is greatly modified as it passes over the South China Sea and the Gulf of Tonkin, arriving over northern Vietnam as a warm, humid air mass. The result is increased rainfall and cloudiness east of the *Chaine Annamite*. This is the period of the *Crachine*, a phenomenon that occurs periodically until spring, generally persisting for two to five days at a time, with clouds 3,000 to 5,000 feet thick. Ceilings are usually below 1,000 feet and frequently below 500 feet. Often there is fog and drizzle or light rain, and visibility is generally reduced to less than two miles and frequently to less than a half-mile.

The transitional periods from late September to early November and from mid-March to mid-May are characterized by changeable weather, bringing frequent showers and thunderstorms as the zone of convergence between the two monsoons transits the area. In the summer, when heavy rains from the southwest monsoon are falling over the southern portion of Indochina, northern Vietnam enjoys its dry season.

Monsoon weather also had an impact on naval operations along the coast, particularly in northern Annam and southern Tonkin, where high seas were produced by winds of the northeast monsoon sweeping across the full reach of the South China Sea. In addition to affecting French amphibious operations, seasonal weather influenced the introduction of communist personnel and materiel into southern Vietnam by sea, their movement from point to point along the coast, and the French attempts to prevent such efforts.

APPENDIX D: ABBREVIATIONS AND ACRONYMS

Aéronavale	Naval Air Arm (French)
Blue water	High seas (Anglo)
BMEO	Far East Naval Brigade
Brown water	Riverine (Anglo)
C in C	Commander in chief
COMAR	Commander Naval Forces
Dinassaut	Naval Infantry Assault Division
DoD	U.S. Department of Defense
FNEO	Naval Forces Far East
FOM	French-designed armed river launch
Fusilier Marin	Naval infantryman
Jeune École	Small navy school of strategy developed in France
Khaki navy	Small ship, working force (those who wore khaki) (French)

APPENDIX D

Landing craft (LC)	Short haul, ship to shore (small) or shore to shore (large), flat-bottom, shallow-draft, self-propelled, ramped barges
Landing ship (LS)	Ocean passage-capable, shore to shore, flat-bottom, shallow-draft, ramped ship
LCA	Landing craft, assault (41 feet long)
LCI	Landing craft, infantry (105 feet long)
LCM	Landing craft, mechanized (56 feet long)
LCM(M)	LCM converted to minesweeper
LCP	Landing craft, personnel (26 to 36 feet long) (became LCVP)
LCT	Landing craft, tank (112 to 192 feet long, depending on country and model)
LCU	Landing craft, utility (port war development) (118 feet long)
LCV	Landing craft, vehicle (36 feet long) (became LCVP)
LCVP	Landing craft, vehicle, personnel (36 feet long)
LSIL	Landing ship, infantry, large (developed as LCIL) (160 feet long)
LSM	Landing ship, medium (204 feet long)
LSSL	Landing ship, support, large (160 feet long) (built on LCIL hull)
LST	Landing ship, tank (288 feet long)
Marine Indochine	French navy in Indochina
Marine Nationale	French navy
MRF	Mobile Riverine Force (U.S.)
Para	Airborne Trooper
POW	Prisoner of War
RAG	River Assault Group (U.S.)
Roi Jean	General de Lattre (nickname)
Rue Royale	The French Navy Ministry, located on that famous street in Paris

APPENDIX D

SNO	Senior Naval Officer (Brit.)
State	U.S. Department of State
SURMAR	Commander Naval Division
Viets	Viet Minh or Viet Cong
VP	French-designed patrol launches (82 feet long)
White navy	Big ship, formal force (those who wore whites) (French)
White water	Estuarine and coastal (Anglo)

APPENDIX E: LIST OF *DINASSAUTS* (SKETCH DATA)

Dinassaut

1: Formed in 1947; based at Hai Duong
2: Formed in 1950; based at Saigon
3: Formed in 1947; based at Nam Dinh
4: Formed in 1947; based first at Vinh Long, then at Ninh Binh
5: Formed in 1947; based at Sept Pagodes
6: Formed in 1947; based at Can Tho and My Tho, then at Vinh Long
8: Formed in 1948; based on aircraft tenders, its commandos and paras specialized in coastal raids
10: Formed in 1950; based at My Tho, operated as a Mekong intervention force
12: Formed in 1952; based at Hanoi

Each *dinassaut* contained an organic light rifle company.

There were in addition three naval commandos: *Jaubert*, *de Montfort*, and *François*. They were organizationally not organic to the *dinassauts*, but worked closely with them.

Temporary *dinassauts* were formed as needed.

APPENDIX F: FRENCH AIRCRAFT CARRIERS

Name	Characteristics	Aircraft
Dixmude CVE	8,200 tons 492.5 feet long 16.5 knots	12 (composite squadron)
Arromanches British CVL	14,000 tons (18,000 full load) 695 feet long 25 knots	30 plus (44 maximum)
La Fayette* CVL	11,000 tons (15,800 full load) 623 feet long 32 knots	26
Bois Belleau* CVL	11,000 tons (15,800 full load) 623 feet long 32 knots	26

*sister ships

BIBLIOGRAPHY

BOOKS

d'Argenlieu, Georges-Thierry. *Chronique d'Indochine 1945–1947.* Paris: Editions Albin Michel, 1985. (The early days' political side.)

Auphan, Paul, et Jacques Mordal. *La Marine Française dans la Seconde Guerre Mondiale.* Paris: Editions France-Empire, 1976. (A standard general work, updated.)

Barjot, Pierre. *Histoire de la Guerre Aéronavale.* Paris: Flammarion, 1961.

Buttinger, Joseph. *The Smaller Dragon: A Political History of Vietnam.* New York: Praeger, 1958.

Cahiers de Louis, Adhémar, Timothée le Golif dit Bornefesse, Capitaine de la Flibuste, 1952. Paris: Grasset, 1952.

Decoux, Jean. *A la barre de l'Indochine.* Paris: Plon, 1949. (Indochina during World War II.)

Devillers, Philippe, and Jean Lacouture. *End of a War: Indochina, 1954.* New York: Praeger, 1969.

Dooley, Thomas A. *Deliver Us from Evil: The Story of Viet Nam's*

Flight to Freedom. New York: Farrar, Straus and Cudahy, 1956.
Ely, Paul. *Indo-China in Turmoil.* Paris: Plon, 1964.
Estival, Bernard. *L'Enseigne dans le Delta.* Versailles: Editions les 7 Vents, 1989. (The final years, seen by a junior officer. Excellent personal insight.)
Fall, Bernard B. *Hell in a Very Small Place: The Siege of Dien Bien Phu.* New York: Lippincott, 1967.
———. *Street without Joy.* Harrisburg, Pa.: Stackpole, 1964.
Forbes, John, and Robert Williams. *Riverine Force.* New York: Bantam, 1987. (A handbook, with photos.)
de Gaulle, Charles. *The Complete War Memories of Charles de Gaulle.* New York: Simon and Schuster, 1959.
Gomane, Jean-Pierre. *Les Marins et l'Outre-Mer.* Paris: Denoël, 1988.
Gras, Yves. *Histoire de la Guerre d'Indochine.* Paris: Plon, 1979.
Gregory, Barry. *Vietnam Coastal and Riverine Forces Handbook.* Wellingborough, England: Patrick Stephens, 1988. (Pictures.)
Gurtov, Melvin. *The First Vietnam Crisis: Chinese Communist Strategy and United States Involvement, 1953–1954.* New York: Columbia University Press, 1967.
Hammer, Ellen J. *The Struggle for Indochina, 1940–1955.* Stanford, Cal.: Stanford University Press, 1954.
Heduy, Philippe, ed. *La Guerre d'Indochine.* Paris: Socièté de Production Littéraire, 1981. (A collection of short essays by key figures and noted experts.)
Ho Chi Minh. *On Revolution: Selected Writings, 1920–66,* ed. Bernard B. Fall. New York: Praeger, 1967.
Hooper, Edwin Bickford. *United States Naval Power in a Changing World.* New York: Praeger, 1988.
Hooper, Edwin B., Dan C. Allard, and Oscar P. Fitzgerald. *The United States Navy and the Vietnam Conflict: The Setting of the Stage to 1959.* Washington, D.C.: Naval History Division, 1976. (Based largely on attaché reports. Good accounts of specific battles.)
Hovey, Harold N. *United States Military Assistance: A Study of Policies and Practices.* New York: Praeger, 1965.
Jane's Fighting Ships. New York: McGraw-Hill, 1945–55. (Naval annual.)
Jaouen, Hervé. *Marin de Guerre.* Paris: Editions du Pen Duick, 1984. (The middle years.)
Kilian, Robert. *History and Memories: The Naval Infantrymen in*

Indochina. Paris: Editions Berger-Levrault, 1948. (BNEO's early commander.)

Lacouture, Jean. *Ho Chi Minh: A Political Biography.* New York: Random House, 1968.

Ladd, J. D. *Assault from the Sea, 1939–45.* London: David & Charles, 1976. (British-oriented descriptions of landing craft development. Includes drawings.)

Lancaster, Donald. *The Emancipation of French Indochina.* London: Oxford University Press, 1961.

Laniel, Joseph. *Le Drame Indochinois de Dien-Bien-Phu au pari de Geneve.* Paris: Plon, 1957.

Mauclère, Jean. *Sailors on the Canals.* Paris: J. Peyronnet, 1950.

McAlister, John T., Jr. *Viet Nam: The Origins of Revolution.* New York: Knopf, 1969.

Michel, Jacques, ed. *La Marine Française en Indochine de 1939 à 1956.* Vincennes: Service Historique de la Marine, 1973–77. Volumes II to V, covering 1945–56. (Invaluable reference.)

Mordal, Jacques. *The Navy in Indochina.* Paris: Amiot-Dumont, 1953. (A standard work.)

Naval History Division. *Riverine Warfare: The U.S. Navy's Operations on Inland Waters.* Washington, D.C.: GPO, 1969.

Naval History Division, eds. *Riverine Warfare: Vietnam.* Washington, D.C.: Office of Chief of Naval Operations, 1972.

Navarre, Henri. *Agony of Indochina.* Paris: Plon, 1957.

O'Ballance, Edgar. *The Indo-China War, 1945–1954: A Study in Guerrilla Warfare.* London: Faber and Faber, 1964.

Polmar, Norman. *Aircraft Carriers: A Graphic History of Carrier Aviation and Its Influence on World Events.* Garden City, N.Y.: Doubleday, 1967.

Power, Thomas F., Jr. *Jules Ferry and the Renaissance of French Imperialism.* New York: Kings Crown Press, 1944.

Reynolds, Clark G. *Command of the Sea: The History and Strategy of Maritime Empires.* New York: Morrow, 1974.

Romé, Paul. *Les Oubliés du Bout du Monde.* Paris: Editions Maritimes & d'Outre-Mer, 1983. (The pre-years.)

Thompson, Robert. *Revolutionary War in World Strategy.* New York: Taplinger, 1970.

Trinquier, Roger. *Modern Warfare.* New York: Praeger, 1964. (Guerrilla war analyzed. As it really was.)

Vo Nguyen Giap. *Banner of People's War: The Party's Military Line.* New York: Praeger, 1970.

———. *The Military Art of People's War: Selected Writings of General Vo Nguyen Giap.* New York: Monthly Review Press, 1970.

Zumwalt, Elmo R. *On Watch.* New York: Quadrangle, 1976.

ARTICLES

de Brossard, Maurice R. "Dinassaut." *La Revue Maritime*, January 1953.

Croizat, Victor J. "Vietnamese Naval Forces: Origin of the Species." *U.S. Naval Institute Proceedings*, February 1973.

Harrigan, Anthony. "River and Shallow-Water Warfare." *Military Review*, October 1965.

———. "Sea and River Guerrillas." *The Canadian Military Journal*, Summer 1965.

Hébert, Guy. "La Naissance d'une Flotilla." *La Revue Maritime*, October 1949.

Heiman, Lee. "River Flotillas of the USSR." *Military Review*, August 1970.

Hess, Gary. "Franklin Roosevelt and Indochina." *Journal of American History*, September 1972.

Julien-Binard, Louis. "Recollections of Nam-Dinh, March 1954." *La Revue Maritime*, December 1956.

La Feber, Walter. "Roosevelt, Churchill and Indochina: 1942–1945." *American Historical Review*, December 1975.

Le Breton, E. "Les Fusiliers Marins en Indochine." *La Revue Maritime*, October 1948.

McClintock, Robert. "The River War in Indochina." *U.S. Naval Institute Proceedings*, December 1954. Also reproduced in *Riverine Warfare: Vietnam*, listed above.

Meyer, Richard M. "The Ground-Sea Team in River Warfare." *Military Review*, September 1966. Also reproduced in *Riverine Warfare: Vietnam*, listed above.

Office of Naval Intelligence. "Development of and Plans for Vietnamese Navy." *The ONI Review*, March 1953.

———. "The Dinassaut Units of Indochina." *The ONI Review*, Supp., Autumn 1952.

———. "French Naval and Air Operations in Indochina." *The ONI Review*, November 1951.

———. "Operations of the French CVL *Arromanches* in Indochina." *The ONI Review*, January 1953.

Ortoli, P. "The French Navy in Indochina." *La Revue Maritime*, December 1952.

Roberts, Chalmers M. "The United States Twice Proposed Indochina Air Strike." *The Washington Post*, 9 July 1954. Reprinted in *The Congressional Record*, Senate, 83rd Congress, 2nd Session, vol. C.

Sabin, Lorenzo S. "South Vietnam—An Exercise in Tragedy." *Shipmate*, April 1965.

Schreadley, Richard L. "The Naval War in Vietnam, 1950–1970." In Uhlig, Frank, ed. *Naval Review, 1971*. Annapolis: U.S. Naval Institute, 1971.

Searle, W. F. "The Case for Inshore Warfare." In Uhlig, Frank, ed. *Naval Review, 1966*. Annapolis: U.S. Naval Institute, 1966.

INDEX

Aéronavale. See Naval Air Arm
Algérien (destroyer escort), 12, 40
Along Bay, 12, 36, 87, 88
Ankhe, 73
Annamite (sloop), xxv, 6
Arquebuse (landing ship, large support), 54
Arromanches (light carrier), 29–30, 48, 70–71, 73
Auboyneau, Philippe-Marie-Joseph-Raymond (vice admiral), xxiv, 20, 82
Audacieuse (armed junk), xxi

Béarn (aircraft transport), xxv, 8, 13
Bien Hoa (airfield), 36

Blanchard, Lieutenant, 11–12
Bois Belleau (light carrier), 40–41, 76–77, 82
Brigade Marine d'Extrême-Orient (BMEO), xxiv, xxv, 1–3, 7, 8, 9–10
British policy, xxii–xxiii, 8, 10, 14, 40
Bui Chu, 58, 85

Campha, 42–43, 86
Camranh Bay, xviii, 36
Can Tho, 6, 57
Cape Camau, 40
Cape St. Jacques, 10–11, 57, 88
Cape Varella, 78
Cat Bi (airfield), 71
Chéliff (landing ship, tank), 77
Chevreuil (sloop), 44, 72

Commandant Dominé (sloop), 73
Commandant Duboc (sloop), 72, 78
Commandant Robert Giraud (seaplane tender), 47, 73, 78
Commando *Jaubert*, 78
Commando *Montfort*, 78, 79
Commentry, Captain André-Jean-Baptiste, *xxi*, *xxv*
Crayssac (armed launch), *xxi*, 11–12
Cu Lao Re Island, 47
Cung Son, 79

d'Argenlieu, Vice Admiral Georges-Thierry, *xxiii*
Decoux, Vice Admiral Jean, *xviii*, *xx*, *xxi*
de Lattre de Tassigny, General Jean, 35–36, 43, 45–46, 48, 49–50
Dévastation (armored barge), 3
dinassauts, 2, 8, 38, 41, 44, 48–49, 51–67, 71, 85–87, 88; craft, 53–57; organization, 53; personnel, 57–59, 87–88; tactics, 26–27, 59–66
Dixmude (escort carrier), 25, 40; compared to *Arromanches*, 29
Doudou (landing craft), 8
Duguay-Trouin (light cruiser), 42, 44
Dumont D'Urville (colonial gunboat), 78

Fai Fo, 25, 78

Fai Tsi Long Islands, *xxi*
Fantasque (destroyer), *xxv*
Far East Naval Brigade. *See Brigade Marine d'Extrême-Orient*
Forces Navales en Extrême-Orient (FNEO). *See* French Navy in Indochina
François, Lieutenant, 21–23
French navy in Indochina: mission, 31–32; organization, 20–21, 27–28, 36–39, 39–40, 52–53; tactics, 28, 39–40, 42, 45, 46–47, 72–73, 78–79
Frézouls (armed launch), *xxi*, 11–12
Fusiliers Marins (naval infantry), 1, 9, 11, 20

Garnier, Lieutenant, 23
Gazelle (sloop), *xxv*, 6
Gian Khau, 26–27
Gloire (light cruiser), *xxv*
Glycine (minesweeper), 30
Gracieuse (sloop), 11
Graziani, Rear Admiral Gaston-Elie, *xxiv*
Gressier barges, 3–4

Haiphong (secondary base), *xviii*, *xix*, 11, 12, 13–14, 18–19, 21–23, 30, 36, 57, 66, 75, 76, 86–87
Hai Van Pass, 24
Haly ("Island of the Dead"), 14
Hanoi, *xix*, *xxii*, 19, 30, 32, 57, 84, 86, 87, 88

INDEX

Hoa Binh, 48
Ho Chi Minh, *xx*, *xxii*, 13–14, 17–18, 26, 31
Hongay, 11, 12
Hué, *xxi*, 24–25, 72, 75
Hung Yen, 64

Jaubert, Commander François, 1–2, 3, 8, 10, 66
Javeline (landing ship, large support), 54

Ké Bao Island, *xxi*
Kilian, Captain Robert, 9

La Capricieuse (sloop), 47, 73
La Fayette (light carrier), 40–41, 82
La Foudre (landing ship dock), 78, 88
Lamotte-Picquet (light cruiser), *xvii*, *xviii*
Langson, *xix*
Lang Tu Vu, 49
Lave (armored barge), 3
Leclerc, Lieutenant General Philippe, *xxiii*, *xxv*, 1, 8
"*les anciens*," *xxiii*
L'Inconstant (sloop), 78

Mao Khe, 43–44
Marcel le Bihan (seaplane tender), 47, 70
Marine Indochine. *See* French navy in Indochina

Marinière (landing craft), 8
Mon Cay, 41–43
My Tho, 4–6, 7, 27, 57

Nam Dinh, 21–24, 58, 85–86
naval air arm, 25, 29–30, 36–37, 40–41, 46–47, 48, 70–71, 73, 78, 79, 82–83
Naval Amphibious Force, 20, 36, 57
Naval Infantry River Flotilla, 4, 10
Navarre, Lieutenant General Henri-Eugène, 74–75
Nha Trang, 6, 76
Ninh Binh, 43–44, 86
north vs. south, 14, 18, 42, 43, 48, 87, 89

Operation *Arethuse*, 78–79
Operation *Atlante*, 77–79
Operation *Auvergne*, 85–87
Operation *Bentré*, 13–14
Operation *Caiman*, 73
Operation *Foudre*, 44–45
Operation *Lea*, 25–26
Operation *Lorraine*, 71–72
Operation *Lotus*, 48–49
Operation *Moussac*, 4–6
Operation *Pirate*, 47
Operation *Saint Sylvestre*, 41–43
Operation *Sauterelle*, 72–73. *See also* Operation *Caiman*
Operation *Toulouse*, 73–74
Ortoli, Vice Admiral Paul-Ange-Philippe, 42, 43, 48

Pertuisane (landing ship, large support), 54
Phat Diem, 58, 85–86
Phudoan, 71
Phu Ly, 86
Phu Quoc Islands, 10
Phu Tho, 71
Phu Yen Binh, 71
Picheral, Lieutenant Commander, *xxiii*
Pnom-Penh, 57
Pontchardier, Lieutenant Commander, 6
Port Wallut, *xxi*, 12
Poulo Condore Island, 10–11
Princess Beatrix (transport), *xxiv*
provisional naval battalion, *xxiii-xxiv*, 3

Queen Emma (transport), *xxiv*
Quercy (transport), *xxv*
Quinhon, 73, 78

Ramatou (landing craft), 8
Rance (landing ship, tank), 41, 78
Rebuffel, Rear Admiral Gabriel-Laurent, 72
Richelieu (fast battleship), *xxiv*, 6, 8, 37
Romé, Lieutenant Paul, 3

Saigon (main base), *xviii*, *xix*, *xxiii*, *xxiv*, *xxv*, 13, 36, 76, 89
Sampanière (landing craft), 8

Savorgnan de Brazza (colonial gunboat), 44, 72
Sénégalais (destroyer escort), *xxv*, 12, 40
Sept Pagodes, 57
Somali (destroyer escort), *xxv*, 12, 40
Sontay, 28
Suffren (heavy cruiser), *xvii*, *xviii*, *xxv*, 24

Thai Binh, 85
Tonnante (armored barge), 3
Tourane, 24–25, 37, 73
Tourville (heavy cruiser), 24
Triomphant (destroyer), *xxiv*, 6, 13
Trung Ha, 48, 71
Tuy Hoa, 78, 79

U.S. military aid, 40–41, 75–77

Vahine (landing craft), 8
Van Fong Lagoon, 74
Van Mon Lagoon, 85
vedettes de patrouille (VPs), 27–28
Vientiane, 57
Viet Minh, *xx*, *xxii*, 14; tactics, 17–19, 26, 28–29, 46, 70, 87, 88, 89
Viet Tri, 71
Vieux Charles (armed junk), *xxi*
Vilar, Lieutenant, 11–12
Ville de Strasbourg (transport), *xxv*

Vinh, 40
Vinh Long, 6
Vinh Yen, 43
Volcan (armored barge), 3

Yenbay–Phu Tho–Tuyenquang
   Triangle, 71

About the Author

CHARLES W. KOBURGER, JR., a captain in the U.S. Coast Guard Reserve, retired in 1978 after 20 years' active duty. He is now an independent consultant in the operational aspects of maritime affairs, specializing in navigation systems. Holder of masters degrees in political science and history, he is also a 1965 graduate of the Armed Forces Staff College. He has been published many times on both sides of the Atlantic. His books are *Sea Power in the Falklands* (Praeger, 1983); *Vessel Traffic Systems* (1986); *The Cyrano Fleet* and *Steel Hulls, Iron Crosses, and Refugees* (both Praeger, 1989); and *Narrow Seas, Small Navies, and Fat Merchantmen* (Praeger, 1990).